MW00582849

# What Works at Historically Black Colleges and Universities (HBCUs)

# What Works at Historically Black Colleges and Universities (HBCUs)

## Nine Strategies for Increasing Retention and Graduation Rates

Tiffany Beth Mfume

ROWMAN & LITTLEFIELD
*Lanham • Boulder • New York • London*

Published by Rowman & Littlefield
A wholly owned subsidiary of The Rowman & Littlefield Publishing Group, Inc.
4501 Forbes Boulevard, Suite 200, Lanham, Maryland 20706
www.rowman.com

Unit A, Whitacre Mews, 26-34 Stannary Street, London SE11 4AB

British Library Cataloguing in Publication Information Available

**Library of Congress Cataloging-in-Publication Data**

Mfume, Tiffany Beth.
  What works at historically Black colleges and universities (HBCUs) : nine strategies for increasing retention and graduation rates / Tiffany Beth Mfume.
    pages cm
  Includes bibliographical references.
  ISBN 978-1-4758-1895-6 (hardcover) — ISBN 978-1-4758-1896-3 (pbk.) — ISBN 978-1-4758-1897-0 (e-book) 1. African American universities and colleges. 2. Academic achievement—United States. 3. College students—Recruiting—United States. 4. College attendance—United States. 5. College dropouts—United States—Prevention. 6. College graduates—United States. I. Title.
  LC2781.M48 2016
  378.7308996073—dc23

                                                                2015030213

∞™ The paper used in this publication meets the minimum requirements of American National Standard for Information Sciences—Permanence of Paper for Printed Library Materials, ANSI/NISO Z39.48-1992.

Printed in the United States of America

# Contents

The Final Impression of First Impressions                    48
Chapter 4: Questions and Next Steps                          49
References                                                   49

**5  Case Management: Systematic Tracking and Monitoring
        of Students by Cohort**                              52
Predictive Analytics                                         53
Why Cohorts?                                                 54
Predicting Success at Morgan                                 55
Navigating the Bill Payment Process                          56
The Origins of Case Management at Morgan                     57
To Drop or Not to Drop—That Is the Question                  58
Education on "Hold"                                          59
Tracking and Monitoring                                      60
Transparent Record Keeping                                   61
"Fishing" for Students                                       61
Case Management: A Proven Strategy                           62
A Winning Combination                                        62
Chapter 5: Questions and Next Steps                          63
References                                                   63

**6  Strategic Initiatives: Programs Designed Specifically to
        "Move the Data"**                                    65
Embrace the System                                           66
Common Academic-Support Programs                             66
Are They Working?                                            67
The Genesis of Strategic Programming at MSU                  68
A Bright Idea Is Born                                        69
The Reclamation Initiative                                   69
The Results Are In. . . .                                    70
A Model Program                                              70
One Step Away                                                71
An Exit Strategy                                             72
Degree-Auditing Software                                     73
Other Strategic Initiatives                                  74
The Genesis of a Philosophy                                  74
Moving the Data                                              74
Becoming and Remaining Strategic                             75
Chapter 6: Questions and Next Steps                          76
References                                                   76

# Acknowledgments

I am grateful that I have been strongly encouraged by my family, my mentors, and my colleagues to forge ahead and "tell my story." First and foremost, I truly thank my partner, my best friend, my mentor, and the "love of my life," my husband, Kweisi Mfume. Honey, your encouragement and support means the world to me; I could never have done this without you!

I sincerely thank my parents, Betha and Lois McMillan, whom I credit with any and all of my professional and personal successes. I am blessed to be the progeny of an English professor and a Mathematics professor who met and fell in love on the campus of Morgan State College in 1970.

I owe this entire book project to my younger sister and book-writing mentor, Dr. Angela McMillan Howell. When Angela published her book in 2013, *Raised Up Down Yonder: Growing Up Black in Rural Alabama*, she set the standard in our family for academic rigor. Thank you, Angela, for your sound wisdom and great advice and for letting me know that I had a book in me, not just a couple of journal articles.

I thank my youngest sister, Sally, my attorney, for her example of strength and courage. Sally, you are a strong, beautiful young woman; I can't wait until you write your book and "tell your story"!

I thank my awesome brother, David, his lovely wife, Jen, and my adorable nephew, James, my favorite brother-in-law, Ricardo, and my wonderful niece (and goddaughter), Lily Isabella Howell. I thank my three amazing sisters-in-law, Darlene, Lawana, and Michelle, and my husband's entire family, especially my fantastic grandchildren.

I have been blessed by a number of mentors who have encouraged me in different ways at different points in my professional career. I thank Dr. John Hudgins at Coppin State University for first opening my eyes to the correct interpretation of data during my graduate program in sociology, for helping me to look beyond the popular data points and examine the truth and reality behind the data, and for asking me every year when I would be writing my book.

I thank Dr. Cecil Payton for having confidence in me and recommending me for the position of director of student retention in 2003. I thank Dr. Maurice Taylor for encouraging me to network with colleagues from across the country, step outside of the "HBCU box," and never neglect my own professional development. I thank my former supervisor, Dr. Nathaniel Knox, for encouraging me to teach in my discipline (public health and health education) so that I could better understand the faculty experience at Morgan State University.

I thank my former supervisor, Dr. Timothy Rainey, for fighting the tough battles for change that served as catalysts for a few major program enhancements at Morgan. I thank my current supervisor, Dr. Kara M. Turner, for holding me to the highest of standards and expecting excellence from me at all times; you are a great leader! I thank both Dr. Earl S. Richardson and Dr. David Wilson, two great HBCU presidents and lovers of Morgan State University.

Finally, I thank my HBCU colleagues with whom I have worked over many years and who are united with me in our pledge to support, uplift, and preserve HBCUs: Dr. John Wolfe, Dr. Joan Langdon, Dr. Anne Gaskins-Nedd, Dr. John Wheatland, Juanita D. Gilliam, Phyllis Brooks Collins, Denyce Watties-Daniels, Robin Leverette Burton, Dr. Thomas James, Dr. Ernesta Pendleton Williams, Grace Mack, Myra Curtis, and Michael James.

I thank my Enrollment Management and Student Academic Support Services (EMSASS) colleagues at Morgan, all under the supervision of associate provost Dr. Kara Turner, Dr. Brenda James, Adrienne Karasik, Hans Cooper, Tanya Wilkerson, Shonda Gray-Cain, and Dr. Darryl Peterkin. "Teamwork makes the dream work!" I sincerely thank my Office of Student Success and Retention (OSSR) staff at Morgan State University, especially my administrative assistant of twelve years, Diane Wise, and my graduate assistant, Simone Durham. You ladies are my right and left arms!

To God be the glory; great things He has done.

# Preface

This book is the culmination of my sixteen years of professional career experience at my alma mater, Morgan State University. After graduating in 1993 with a bachelor's degree in biology, I returned to Morgan State University to work as an academic advisor in the Academic Development Center on June 1, 1999. Never did I imagine that I would grow into a seasoned professional in the field of student success, retention, persistence, and degree completion in higher education over the course of sixteen years of employment and professional development at Morgan State University.

As a product of a historically black university, I am a believer that both the best and brightest students, and students who have yet to demonstrate their true potential, can thrive and be developed at America's HBCUs.

During my tenure at Morgan State University, I have participated in many new initiatives, self-studies, and innovative programs to promote student success. It has been a process of "hit and miss" and "trial and error" that has resulted in a success model at Morgan that HBCUs and other institutions of higher education can study and emulate.

Often, one of the legitimate criticisms of HBCUs is our failure to document and publish our programs, initiatives, and models of success. I have attended workshops, conferences, seminars, forums, summits, and symposia along with a few of my colleagues at other HBCUs, only for us to find ourselves greatly outnumbered by colleagues from majority institutions who present and publish detailed findings with concrete recommendations and implications for student success.

In any literature review pertaining to retention and graduation rates, degree completion, student persistence, or student success, a vacuity of information from HBCUs is the norm. This is especially true on a large scale. For example, there are articles and publications that highlight student success initiatives for small subpopulations or specific student groups at HBCUs with only twenty to two hundred student participants, but there is limited literature on full-scale, whole-campus models at large, public HBCUs with over five thousand students.

I have known for at least eight out of my sixteen years at Morgan that I should be publishing the results of our efforts to increase retention and graduation rates. Even though I had become very skilled at making public presentations at conferences over the years, I still had failed to publish these presentations. In fact, one of the "hot topics" at every HBCU conference is always our own admonishment to come back the following year with a plan to publish and document our results. And even though many HBCUs participate in comprehensive studies and nationwide success models, our stories usually are told from the outside looking in. I knew that I wanted to present a case study documented from the inside looking out.

All of the data presented in this book is public information that has been reported to the U.S. Department of Education (IPEDS) and/or the Maryland Higher Education Commission (MHEC), reported to outside grantors and external funding agencies, or reported via the Morgan State University website. This book provides a compilation of existing data at Morgan State University presented in the context of a comprehensive student success case study.

I am delighted and honored to present our work at Morgan State University and frame it in the context of current literature and research in higher education, as well as in the context of the present public perception of HBCUs. I share with the readers of this book some of my personal stories as examples to support my larger concepts. These stories represent my perceptions and recollections of the events that have influenced, impacted, and shaped our success model at Morgan State University.

It is my intention to have this book serve as a manual, a guide for HBCUs, and colleges and universities in the nation, to study, motivate, and inspire effective, data-driven strategies and innovations; it is written to promote student success, and ultimately to help increase retention and graduation rates. Many times we, as faculty, staff, and administrators at HBCUs, are guilty of working so diligently to foster success through student engagement and hard work on a day-to-day basis that we neglect to document our successes and write our own narrative.

# Introduction

## *HBCUs: Legacy and Historical Context*

In 2011, Morgan State University, one of four public historically black colleges and universities (HBCUs) in the state of Maryland, increased its retention rate from 67 percent to 73 percent and its graduation rate from 28 percent to 34 percent. And after three consecutive years (2011–2013) with a retention rate above 72 percent, in fall 2014 the retention rate for the 2013 freshman cohort was *76.3 percent*, Morgan's highest retention rate in twenty years and the second highest retention rate in Morgan's history.

This was achieved through a combination of early intervention strategies, systematic tracking and monitoring, and academic coaching and mentoring. But there is far more to it than that; after working in student success at Morgan State University for sixteen years, and eleven years as director of student retention, one administrator has observed and recognized that it took much fine-tuning, tweaking, and the right combination of programs and strategies to achieve and maintain these results. And, after having made dozens of presentations at conferences, summits, workshops, and symposia in reference to Morgan's increased retention and graduation rates, one question frequently has been asked, "How was it done?" and more importantly, "How have these results been maintained?"

The answer is not a "quick fix," nor is the answer found in any existing article or textbook in the field of higher education. In fact, there is little documentation on successful, large-scale retention and graduation strategies at HBCUs that is authored by the faculty, staff, or administrators within these institutions. What is found in a review of the recent literature instead is that many of the more than one hundred HBCUs in the United States are fighting for survival, struggling to prove their relevance in a "post-racial" society.

According to the National Conference of State Legislatures, twenty-five states have a funding formula in place that allocates some amount of public funding based on performance indicators such as course completion, time to degree, transfer rates, the number of degrees awarded, or the number of low-income and minority graduates. Five additional states are currently transitioning to some type of performance-based funding; this means that the legislature or governing board has approved a performance-funding program and the details are currently being worked out.

Now more than ever, HBCUs, especially public HBCUs, find themselves in the "hot seat" and "under the gun" with the need to show proven results. The six-year graduation rate at HBCUs averages approximately 30 percent, and, "within the body of research on HBCUs, there are few studies that examine how institutional behavior and financial strategies (such as the allocation of resources) influence retention and graduation rates" (Lee, 2012, p. ii). Thus, Morgan's "recipe" for student success provides a model for HBCUs and institutions of higher education who serve minority student populations to study, discuss, and potentially emulate.

## HBCUS: HISTORICAL CONTEXT

According to the Postsecondary National Policy Institute, HBCUs can be defined as higher education institutions established prior to 1964 whose primary mission is to educate African-Americans. Many of these institutions were founded and developed post-slavery and during segregation when most postsecondary institutions were not open to people of color.

The first HBCU, Cheyney University in Pennsylvania, was founded in 1837. When the U.S. Congress passed the Morrill Land-Grant Act in 1862 giving federal land to states for the purpose of opening colleges and universities to educate farmers, scientists, and teachers, only Alcorn State University in Mississippi was open to African-Americans and designated as a black land-grant college.

The majority of HBCUs were founded as private institutions until 1890 when the passage of the second Land-Grant Act required states to open their land-grant institutions to black students or allocate funding to black institutions that could serve as alternatives to white institutions. This resulted in sixteen new HBCUs open only to people of color, most of them public institutions. The federal government's Freedmen's Bureau, black churches, and the American Missionary Association founded many of the additional institutions that would later become HBCUs.

Today, the White House Initiative on HBCUs declares that all 105 HBCUs offer all students, regardless of race, an opportunity to develop their skills and talents. The National Center for Education Statistics (NCES) reports that the number of students enrolled at HBCUs rose by 45 percent between 1976 and 2011, from 223,000 to 324,000. According to NCES data in 2011, HBCUs enroll 11 percent of African-American students in the United States, even though HBCUs constitute less than 3 percent of colleges and universities in the nation. A list of accredited HBCUs is presented in appendix A.

HBCUs graduate nearly 25 percent of African-Americans who earn undergraduate degrees in the United States. Specifically, "over half of all African-American professionals are graduates of HBCUs, nine of the top ten colleges that graduate the most African-Americans who go on to earn PhDs are HBCUs, and more than 50 percent of the nation's African-American public school teachers and 70 percent of African-American dentists earned degrees at HBCUs" (Knight, Davenport, Green-Powell & Hilton, 2012, p. 227).

A 2006 report, *Economic Impact of the Nation's Historically Black Colleges and Universities*, recorded several key findings about the immeasurable impact of HBCUs: the 101 HBCUs in 2001 collectively generated a value-added (or gross regional product) impact of $6 billion; public HBCUs accounted for 62 percent of this total amount while not-for-profit HBCUs accounted for the remaining 38 percent in terms of output (revenues); and in 2001 the nation's HBCUs would have ranked 232nd on the Forbes Fortune 500 list of the United States' largest companies.

## MORGAN STATE UNIVERSITY: A BRIEF HISTORY

Founded in 1867 as the Centenary Biblical Institute by the Baltimore Conference of the Methodist Episcopal Church, the institution's original mission was to train young men for the ministry. It subsequently broadened its mission to educate both men and women as teachers. It was renamed Morgan College in 1890 in honor of the Reverend Lyttleton Morgan, the first chairman of its Board of Trustees, who donated land to the college. Morgan remained a private institution until 1939. In that year, the state of Maryland purchased the institution in response to a study by a state commission that found that Maryland needed to provide more opportunities for its black citizens. The name became Morgan State College.

In the mid-1960s, the Middle States Association of Colleges and Schools cited Morgan as a model liberal arts campus. In 1975, the state legislature designated Morgan as a public urban university, gave it the authority to offer doctorates, and enabled the institution to have its own governing board. In 1988, Maryland reorganized its higher education structure and created the Maryland Higher Education Commission to coordinate the growth and development of postsecondary education in Maryland.

Morgan State University has a history of serving individuals from under-represented minority backgrounds and, consequently, it gives priority to ad-dressing the needs of the populations of the urban community. Morgan's mis-sion is to serve a multiethnic and multiracial student body and to help ensure that the benefits of higher education are enjoyed by a broad segment of the population. In 2007, Morgan State University was classified by the Carnegie Foundation as a doctoral research institution. Morgan prepares and develops scientists, engineers, and scholars in all other disciplines to conduct research and development for industry, government, and universities.

Currently, Morgan is first among traditional campuses in Maryland in the number of bachelor's degrees awarded to African-Americans; first among all campuses in Maryland and among the top ten campuses nationwide in the number of doctorates awarded to African-Americans; first among minority-serving institutions (MSIs) nationally in the number of Fulbright scholars graduated; first among MSIs nationwide in the number of Fulbright scholars on faculty; first among HBCUs nationwide in the number of Fulbright schol-ars graduated; and first among HBCUs nationwide in Fulbright scholars on faculty.

Morgan State University has been listed by *U.S. News & World Report* as "one of students' most popular universities" and named by *Forbes* magazine among "America's Best Colleges and Universities." Additionally, Morgan has been identified as "one of the 25 Best Universities for African-Americans, Hispanics, and Women" by the *Black EOE Journal, Hispanic Network* maga-zine, and *Professional Woman's* magazine. In January 2015, Morgan State University was cited in *U.S. News & World Report* magazine as "one of the top 12 HBCUs where freshmen return."

## MORGAN'S OFFICE OF STUDENT SUCCESS AND RETENTION

In 2003, Morgan State University created the Office of Student Retention, presently known as the Office of Student Success and Retention (OSSR), which is housed in the division of Academic Affairs under the provost. The purpose of the OSSR is to work in collaboration with the College of Liberal Arts, the School of Engineering, the School of Computer, Mathematical and Natural Sciences, the Earl G. Graves School of Business and Management, the School of Education and Urban Studies, the School Community Health and Policy, the School of Architecture and Planning, the School of Social Work, the School of Global Journalism and Communication, and the various academic support programs of the university to provide continuous, high-quality support for undergraduate students from matriculation to graduation.

The goal of this comprehensive retention program is to increase student retention rates and persistence to graduation with a focus on academic success and achievement through early intervention and systematic tracking of undergraduate students. While Morgan State University has consistently graduated undergraduate students at the expected rates based on predictive modeling, the vision of the OSSR is to graduate students at higher rates than would be expected based on students' precollege preparation and their financial circumstances.

The OSSR works to produce graduates of Morgan State University who are well prepared to meet the challenges of internship, graduate school, professional school, and career following their successful matriculation and graduation from the institution.

To that end, the OSSR employs twenty dedicated staff including a director of student success and retention. Since its inception in 2003, Morgan State University's OSSR has:

- implemented a campus-wide retention program with retention coordinators for every school;
- completely revamped freshman orientation for new students from an optional, more social transitional program for freshmen to a mandatory academic, social, and cultural transitional program for all freshmen;
- developed a comprehensive student retention website;
- coordinated participation in a five-year longitudinal study (the Collegiate Learning Assessment) to measure "value added" to Morgan students;
- partnered with the White House Initiative on HBCUs and the FDIC to provide a comprehensive financial literacy program utilizing the FDIC's MoneySmart financial literacy curriculum and won the Maryland DC Campus Compact (MDCCC) AmeriCorps*VISTA grant to employ a full-time AmeriCorps*VISTA volunteer in the position of financial literacy coordinator for three years;
- initiated the Parents' 411 program for parents and families of Morgan undergraduate students including the *Parents' 411* newsletter published at least once per academic year and the Parents' 411 orientation program convened during the summer orientation (the ACCESS Orientation Program) for first-time freshmen;
- published Morgan's first university guide for new and prospective students, parents, and families;
- managed all aspects of university placement testing including the conversion of the university placement testing system from ETS to Accuplacer, the purchasing of test units, the selection of cut-off scores, the determination of course placement, and the dissemination of results;

- assumed responsibility (for seven years) for providing reasonable accommodations for students with disabilities and created the Student Accessibility Support Services Program (SASS Program);
- launched a new "Reclamation" Initiative creating opportunities for students who leave the university in good academic standing to return in their fifth or sixth academic year to finish Morgan "on time" in six consecutive years or less;
- been awarded a $100,000 grant from the Bill & Melinda Gates Foundation for the implementation of Integrated Planning and Advising Services (IPAS) technology;
- implemented Starfish Retention Solutions to enhance advising and provide sophisticated, yet user-friendly tracking and monitoring systems for the university; and
- won a grant to fund a comprehensive degree-auditing system (Degree Works by Ellucian) that will promote degree completion by providing easy access to interactive, "live" degree plans for students, faculty, and advisors.

The work of the OSSR will be presented throughout this book, highlighting specific examples of programs and initiatives associated with each of the nine strategies to improve retention and graduation rates.

## WHO IS THIS BOOK FOR?

Many of the current books in the field of higher education are more theoretical and/or philosophical and less practical, or they are more specific in nature and do not deliver broad-based approaches and strategies to increase retention and graduation rates, or the perspective of authors is from the outside of an institution looking in rather than from the inside looking out.

This book aims to stimulate discussion in any classroom, at any conference, or simply over the dinner table between two professionals after a long day at the office. Any professional can relate to one or more of the challenges and/or limitations in the field of higher education that this book addresses.

This book is written from three distinct vantage points: the personal perspective of an administrator with sixteen years of professional experience at an HBCU, the evidence and data-driven approach to student success in higher education, and as a case study of the student success model at Morgan State University, a public HBCU in Maryland. Each book chapter includes personal "vignettes" as sidebars, in addition to "next steps" at the end of the chapter with reflective questions and a short list of next-step action items.

The reader of this book is introduced to storytelling, coupled with data and best practices to undergird the stories, plus "real-life" examples of the implementation of specific programs and initiatives at Morgan State University. After reading this book, readers will walk away with new programming ideas to actually implement and test at other postsecondary institutions, with specific lessons learned and best practices to promote student success, as well as with insight into leadership and decision making in higher education.

This book can serve as both a professional reference for any faculty, staff, or administrator working in postsecondary education, as well as a supplemental textbook for all of the growing graduate programs in the field of higher education. *What Works at Historically Black Colleges and Universities (HBCUs): Nine Strategies for Increasing Retention and Graduation Rates* is appropriate for any graduate-level course in the field of higher education including courses such as Contemporary Issues in Higher Education, Governance and Administration of Higher Education, Applied Social Research, Historical Foundations of Higher Education, Issues and Problems at Urban and Special Mission Institutions, Student Development Theory, and many other master's and doctoral-level courses.

## WHAT IS THIS BOOK ABOUT?

This book begins with chapter 1, "Leadership: You Are Only as Good as Your College President," which details the critical importance of executive leadership at HBCUs. For the past thirty-plus years at Morgan State University, two very different but effective leaders have presided over the campus. Too many HBCUs have retained interim or acting presidents, presidents who are at odds with governing boards, faculty, and/or campus constituents, or presidents who simply are not effective, productive leaders. Chapter 1 discusses senior leadership at HBCUs and suggests "next steps" for student success administrators to support and positively impact senior leadership at an institution.

Chapter 2 challenges the reader to assign a corporate-style "brand" to an HBCU, one that will be true to the identity and actuality of what the institution offers to students and to the campus community at large.

Chapter 3 reminds the reader of the power of data and how understanding student data and student characteristics should drive strategic student retention programs and initiatives.

Chapter 4 reinforces Vincent Tinto's (1993) theory that institutions should frontload their efforts on behalf of student retention. Chapter 4 proposes that frontloading by allocating resources (both financial and human resources) to summer, transition, and first-year programs is critically important at HBCUs where resources are often scarce.

Chapter 5 explains the highly successful case-management approach at Morgan where OSSR staff track and systematically monitor students who fail to make satisfactory payment arrangements by the deadline, students who fail to register for courses by the deadline, and students who earn grades of D, F, I, or W at midterm or final. These students represent Morgan's "at-risk" cohorts of students. The increase in Morgan's retention and graduation rates can be attributed, in part, to this approach to intervening with "at-risk" cohorts.

Chapter 6 suggests that institutions design programs that "on purpose" increase retention and graduation rates. One example is the Reclamation Initiative, now in its fifth year of implementation, which creates opportunities for students who leave Morgan in good academic standing to return in their fifth or sixth academic year to finish Morgan "on time" in six consecutive years or less.

Chapter 7 places emphasis on the power of external grants and funding. A "game-changer" at Morgan State University has been the $100,000 grant from the Bill & Melinda Gates Foundation for the implementation of Integrated Planning and Advising Services (IPAS) technology. As one of only nineteen selected institutions and the only HBCU, Morgan has partnered with Starfish Retention Solutions to automate its Early Alert and Response System (EARS) for faculty, staff, and students. Most importantly, the IPAS grant provided the opportunity, the initial financial resources, and an external push to effectuate a campus-wide culture change at Morgan.

Chapter 8 establishes how tools such as Google Apps, Starfish, Degree Works, and Smarthinking help administrators, faculty, and staff to work smarter by using existing technology.

Chapter 9 encourages readers to network by presenting research at conferences, communicating with colleagues, and sharing successes and failures with the HBCU community; through this exchange of ideas and best practices, we learn and grow our institutions.

Chapter 10 reviews "the recipe" for student success at HBCUs by putting all of the ingredients together and showing how they are interrelated and complementary to each other in the end and ultimately increase retention and graduation rates.

*What Works at Historically Black Colleges and Universities (HBCUs): Nine Strategies for Increasing Retention and Graduation Rates* will have broad appeal within the field of education and beyond. While the primary audience for this book is the faculty, staff, administrators, students, alumni, and campus community of the current 105 HBCUs in the United States, this book is written to appeal to all professionals in the field of higher education, guidance counselors and administrators in K–12 education, sociologists and social scientists, and scholars who study change management, outcomes assessment, and success in any organized structure or system.

## REFERENCES

Gasman, M. (2013). *The Changing Face of Historically Black Colleges and Universities.* Philadelphia: Center for Minority Serving Institutions, University of Pennsylvania.

Humphreys, J. (2006). Economic Impact of the Nation's Historically Black Colleges and Universities (NCES 2007-178). U.S. Department of Education, National Center for Education Statistics. Washington, DC: U.S. Government Printing Office.

Knight, L., Davenport, E., Green-Powell, P., & Hilton, A. A. (2012). The Role of Historically Black Colleges or Universities in Today's Higher Education Landscape. *International Journal of Education, 4*(2), 223–35.

Lee, K. (2012). An Analysis of the Institutional Factors that Influence Retention and 6-Year Graduation Rates at Historically Black Colleges and Universities. Available at http://hdl.handle.net/10161/5244.

National Center for Education Statistics. (2011). Institute of Education Sciences, U.S. Department of Education, Integrated Postsecondary Education Data System (IPEDS).

Postsecondary National Policy Institute. (2015). *Historically Black Colleges and Universities (HBCUs): A Background Primer.* Available at www.newamerica.org/postsecondary-national-policy-institute/historically-black-colleges-and-universities-hbcus.

Tinto, V. (1994). Toward a Theory of Doctoral Persistence. *Leaving College: Rethinking the Causes and Cures of Student Attrition.* Chicago: University of Chicago Press, 230–43.

Tinto, V. (1999). Taking Retention Seriously: Rethinking the First Year of College. *NACADA Journal, 19*(2), 5–9.

*Chapter One*

# Leadership

## *You Are Only as Good as Your College President*

It is not difficult to survey any news outlet or publication and notice HBCU presidents featured in the headlines. Departures, untimely exits, retirements, new appointments, transitions, and interim and acting presidencies are commonplace in the HBCU narrative. According to the White House Initiative on Historically Black Colleges and Universities November 2014 listing of the 105 HBCU presidents, thirteen of the presidents (12 percent) are serving in an interim or acting capacity. While HBCU presidents serve for less time than the national average, six years compared to 8.5 years nationally, an elite group of HBCU presidents serve long terms between fifteen and twenty-five years (Freeman & Gasman, 2014; Gasman, 2013).

This variation in tenure from one extreme—the interim or acting presidency—to the other extreme—the twenty-year-plus presidency—has embedded challenges for administrators, faculty, staff, and students at both ends. How can an institution promote student success and seek to increase retention and graduation rates in the face of leadership that often may be fluctuating or sometimes perhaps remaining stagnant? This chapter provides strategies to promote student success in the context of the HBCU presidency and institutional leadership.

## THE COLLEGE PRESIDENCY IN AMERICA: A PROFILE

The American College President Study: Key Findings and Takeaways, the American Council on Education's (ACE) seventh report in the American

College President Study series, provides insight into the past, present, and future of college presidencies in America. The ACE report has found:

> Two decades ago, the average age of college and university presidents was 52. Today, it is 61. In fact, in 1986 just 13 percent of presidents were over the age of 60. In 2011, 58 percent of presidents are over 60. One possible reason for this aging of the presidency is the increasing complexity of leading a postsecondary institution. As colleges and universities face a growing number of internal and external challenges, governing boards and search committees are likely looking for more experienced leaders. This tenet is supported by the fact that 54 percent of current presidents in 2011 were presidents in their last position. In 1986, only 40 percent of sitting presidents held a presidency in their previous role. (Cook, 2012)

The comprehensive ACE study further concludes that "rapidly ballooning enrollments, escalating fiscal pressures, the change engines of technological advances, a wide array of constituents, and a tumultuous political climate all make it more important than ever for college and university presidents to understand and be responsive to their communities and the contexts in which higher education takes place" (Cook, 2012).

The author cautions that while institutions may prefer older leaders with proven track records in similar positions, this preference works to the disadvantage of younger leaders, women, and minorities. And anticipated mass retirements of "Baby Boomers" may leave a temporary shortage of leadership.

## HBCU PRESIDENTS: THE BEST OF THE "OLD GUARD"

Arguably, one of the best HBCU presidents ever is Dr. Benjamin Elijah Mays, president of Morehouse College for twenty-seven years from 1940 until 1967. Dr. Mays was known for his uncompromising positions on human rights and democracy. At Morehouse, Dr. Mays bolstered the academic reputation of the institution, secured institutional funding and student financial support, and expanded institutional infrastructure (Rovaris, 2005). Hundreds, perhaps thousands, of Morehouse alumni (including Rev. Dr. Martin Luther King Jr.) have cited Dr. Benjamin E. Mays as a personal mentor who left an indelible impression on their lives.

Dr. Norman C. Francis and Xavier University are practically synonymous and interchangeable. Dr. Francis has been the president of Xavier University since 1968, for forty-seven years, making him the longest-sitting university president in the United States. "Since he took the helm in 1968, enrollment at Xavier has nearly tripled. The campus has expanded from five permanent buildings covering the size of a city block to 16 permanent buildings spread across 60 manicured acres. The school's endowment has surged from $20 million to more than $130 million today" (Lipinski, 2014).

After announcing his retirement in September 2014, at age 83, Dr. Francis left a legacy at Xavier University, which includes rebounding from an unprecedented setback after Hurricane Katrina with an enrollment that dropped from four thousand students in fall 2005, to five hundred students five months after Hurricane Katrina, to now an enrollment of more than 3,200 students in 2015. Dr. Francis's leadership shepherded the institution through this natural disaster without the university ever closing its doors.

Dr. William R. Harvey has been the president of Hampton University (HU) since 1978, bringing more than seventy-five new academic programs to Hampton during his tenure of thirty-six-plus years. Under his leadership, Hampton's enrollment has increased from 2,700 students to more than 6,300 students with an average SAT score (combined math and verbal) of entering freshman increasing by approximately three hundred points. Dr. Harvey's commitment to the academic excellence and success of HU has been undergirded by his personal commitment to the students, faculty, and staff of Hampton University.

In 2014, Dr. Harvey gave a $108,403 personal gift to HU to support a wage increase for all (121) full-time permanent HU staff earning less than $9 an hour (Keierleber, 2014). President Harvey made two similar donations to Hampton University in the past; in June 2011, he donated $166,000 to increase staff wages to $8 an hour, and in May 2011, Dr. Harvey donated $1 million to HU to be utilized as incentives to increase faculty salaries. This was in addition to the $1 million that he contributed in 2001 to provide scholarships to students who wanted to become teachers.

## HBCU PRESIDENTS: THE BEST OF THE "NEW SCHOOL"

As Dr. Beverly Daniel Tatum approaches the end of her presidency at Spelman College in 2015 after twelve years of leadership, her leadership style could easily be considered both "old guard" and "new school." The length of her tenure (lasting double the average length of an HBCU presidency) may suggest "old guard" style commitment and dedication, but Dr. Tatum began her presidency in her forties and brought a "new school" sense of vision and innovation with her to the campus of Spelman College.

Most notably, Dr. Tatum launched a fundraising campaign to increase scholarship support for students, provide additional investment in faculty and academic programs, and complete capital improvement projects on campus that raised a record-setting $157.8 million over the duration of its ten-year span. The funding generated by the campaign is the largest amount raised in the history of the institution and was supported by twelve thousand (71 percent) alumni donors (Davis, 2014).

In 2013, Dr. Tatum was the first and only HBCU president to win the Carnegie Corporation's Academic Leadership Award, which honors university presidents who not only are resourceful administrators and managers but also have a keen interest in the liberal arts and a commitment to excellence and access, curricular innovation, reform of K–12 education, international engagement, and the promotion of strong links between their institutions and their local communities. This award for an outstanding college president in the United States is accompanied by $500,000 donation from the Carnegie Corporation to be invested in any of the honoree's academic initiatives.

During Dr. Walter Kimbrough's seven-year presidency at Philander Smith College in Little Rock, Arkansas, he adopted a social justice mission for the institution, created the legendary "Bless the Mic: A Hip Hop President's Lecture Series," raised the retention rate to 77 percent, corrected the institution's operations, improved faculty pay and fostered faculty development, increased alumni giving from 4 percent to nearly 16 percent, launched a black male initiative, and improved energy efficiency, among other accomplishments (Gasman, 2012).

What made Dr. Kimbrough's presidency at Philander Smith a "game-changer" in the HBCU landscape was not just these accomplishments, but his effectiveness in changing perceptions and raising the profile of the HBCU presidency overall through both social media and his writings in blogs, editorials, and commentaries. In 2011, he penned "Black Colleges Still Play a Vital Role in Education" in the *Chronicle of Higher Education*. Dr. Kimbrough has been an unashamed, bold advocate for the relevance and ongoing necessity of HBCUs in American higher education. He became affectionately known as the "Hip Hop Prez" by students who found that they could relate to his leadership style.

Now in his third year of presidency at Dillard University, Dr. Kimbrough's leadership has seen enrollment at Dillard increase to twelve hundred students in 2015 and the number of presidential scholars at the institution also has increased. Dr. Kimbrough hosts the "Brain Food" lecture series at Dillard, he is celebrating the fiftieth anniversary of the Upward Bound program at Dillard, and he has announced Denzel Washington as the 2015 commencement speaker at Dillard, one of the highest-profile commencement speakers in Dillard's history.

Michael Sorrell, Esq., brought his reputation as a "fixer" to the campus of Paul Quinn College in 2007. One journalist wrote of Michael Sorrell's inspiring presidency, "Dallas' only historically black college [Paul Quinn] was on the brink of collapse. Now the students are protesters, the football field is a farm, and the president is a star" (Howard, 2012).

Since taking over leadership at Paul Quinn College, President Sorrell has demolished fifteen abandoned buildings from the 146-acre campus, improved admission standards, secured accreditation, eliminated the football team, increased the graduation rate, enforced a new dress code for the entire campus, recruited a mostly new faculty and staff, increased partnerships and donor bases, and created an urban farm on what was once the football field.

President Sorrell has been successful in rebranding the institution, labeling all Paul Quinn students as "Quinnites." After initially having to cut salaries for a whole year, including his own salary by 25 percent, the vice presidents' salaries by 20 percent, directors' salaries by 15 percent, and faculty salaries by 10 percent, President Sorrell now boasts an annual budget surplus of more than $2 million (Howard, 2012). President Sorrell uses Twitter, Facebook, and Instagram to promote the agenda of the institution, to disseminate exciting "Quinnite" news, and to increase stakeholder buy-in both on and off campus.

## MORGAN STATE UNIVERSITY: A TALE OF TWO PRESIDENTS

In the sixteen years that I have been employed at Morgan State University, I've had the privilege to work under two outstanding HBCU college presidents, Dr. Earl S. Richardson and Dr. David Wilson. I have been granted the opportunity to observe their two very different leadership styles.

Dr. Richardson is a great example of the "old guard" of HBCU leadership. Over the course of Dr. Richardson's twenty-six-year presidency at Morgan, he presided over a Morgan State University "rebirth and renaissance" to include more than $400 million in campus renovations and construction. Not only did the campus expand exponentially physically, but also enrollment surged under his leadership from thirty-six hundred students when he became president in 1984 to more than seven thousand students at the time of his retirement in 2010. One of his greatest accomplishments was his role in upgrading Morgan's Carnegie Foundation classification to "doctoral research university."

It was an honor for me to travel to Annapolis, Maryland, for legislative sessions and to take note of Dr. Richardson's masterful command of storytelling. He always brought with him Morgan students to testify before the legislature and budget committees. I witnessed legislators become emotional as they listened to Dr. Richardson, in the tradition of a seasoned griot, lead them through individual examples of students' resilience, perseverance, and persistence to degree completion. His masterful command of storytelling often led him "off script" as he shared with legislators compelling and engaging examples of student success and tenacity to support his fiscal agenda for the year.

In 2010, Dr. David Wilson arrived on Morgan's campus, a Harvard-educated product of "the Academy" who found himself returning to "his roots" in service to young black youth just as he had been served as an undergraduate at Tuskegee University. President Wilson's style and approach were different; his tone was more formal, and he brought with him a new vision and slogan for the university: "Growing the Future, Leading the World."

Under his "new school" style leadership, Morgan State University became the first HBCU to offer a MOOC (massive open online course). Dr. Wilson has brokered partnerships with Saudi Arabia, Brazil, and China to promote study abroad as well as to bring international students to Morgan's campus. When I have traveled to legislative hearings in Annapolis with President Wilson, his approach has been to flood legislators with data points and facts all pointing to the unequivocal relevance of and need for Morgan to provide innovation and leadership in Maryland.

Instead of bringing students to the legislative hearings to tell their stories, Dr. Wilson has initiated an annual Morgan Innovation Day in Annapolis where our students and faculty showcase their research and innovation through interactive posters and presentations. The differences in the "old guard" and "new school" leadership styles of these two great men represent the best of the HBCU presidency, past, present, and future.

## "OLD GUARD" VERSUS "NEW SCHOOL"

What do the "old guard" college presidents (Dr. Benjamin E. Mays, Dr. Norman C. Francis, Dr. William R. Harvey, and Dr. Earl S. Richardson) and the "new school" college presidents (Dr. Beverly Daniel Tatum, Dr. Walter Kimbrough, Mr. Michael Sorrell, Esq., and Dr. David Wilson) have in common that has led to their successful tenures as president of HBCUs? Although their leadership styles may differ, certain commonalities exist.

The components of excellent HBCU leadership as exemplified by these "old guard" and "new school" figures are:

1. focusing on student success and improving student success benchmarks such as retention and graduation rates;
2. excelling at fundraising and budgeting;
3. navigating the politics of governance and boards;
4. strengthening academic programs;
5. engaging with faculty;
6. fostering alumni engagement;
7. making tough decisions that aren't always popular; and
8. making personal sacrifices that include pay cuts or financial donations if needed.

Most importantly, these presidents have served as great ambassadors for their institutions, using their charisma and communication skills to promote the success of HBCUs.

## NAVIGATING CHANGES IN SENIOR LEADERSHIP

If, as the title of this chapter suggests, "you are only as good as your college president" and senior leadership at an institution drives the strategic direction of an institution, then what can be done to increase retention and graduation rates in the context of leadership that may be fluctuating or stagnant? Because college presidents balance an interdependent combination of institutional leadership and organizational management, strategies for affecting their decision making can be employed by campus constituents (Taylor & Machado, 2006). Three specific strategies for affecting the decision making of senior leadership are promoting a culture of evidence on campus, cultivating respectful, professional relationships on campus, and employing good timing and preparation.

The first strategy to positively influence senior leadership is to promote a culture of evidence on campus. A good leader, a seasoned college president or a newly appointed college president, will appreciate being approached by campus constituents in the context of evidence-based and outcomes-driven strategic planning. Fullan and Scott, authors of *Turnaround Leadership for Higher Education,* assert that "turnaround leaders reach out to those who will make a desired change work with a well-argued, evidence-based case on why action in this area is necessary" (2009, p. 99). All student success ideas, programs, and initiatives should be framed by data and evidence. Great leaders care less about opinions and personal observations and more about effective strategies and data-driven outcomes.

A second strategy to positively influence senior leadership is to cultivate respectful, professional relationships on campus. Often, before a new president arrives on campus, certain faculty, staff, and administrators already have been labeled as difficult, renegade, or rogue. The college president should be the first positive, respectful relationship that an administrator or staff member cultivates on campus. "Likewise, administrators tend to recognize their organization's culture only when they have transgressed its bounds and severe conflicts or adverse relationships ensue . . . and organizational culture is dealt with in an atmosphere of crisis management, instead of reasoned reflection and consensual change" (Tierney, 1988, p. 4).

Approach is everything; even when disagreements occur and dissenting opinions exist between colleagues, a tone of professional respect and courtesy must be maintained. Leadership routinely works through a series of dialectical relationships often arising from the juxtaposition of conflicting ideas, forces, and differentials of power and resources (Collinson, 2005). College presidents should not have to spend too much time sorting through personalities instead of understanding functionalities.

A third strategy to positively influence senior leadership is to employ good timing and preparation. As outlined previously in this chapter, the demands on HBCU presidents are myriad. Everyone wants "the president's ear" to share suggestions, criticisms, recommendations, ideas, and innovations; however, there is insufficient time for a college president to grant a meeting and/or presentation to every campus administrator, constituent, or stakeholder who seeks to have audience with the president. If an opportunity to speak with the president arises, new ideas, proposals, and recommendations already should be finalized, vetted, and truncated and ready for presentation without notice.

## NEW LEADERSHIP = NEW OPPORTUNITIES

When I became the director of student retention at Morgan State University in 2003, I began working with an appointed campus-wide Retention Advisory Committee to identify what we called "Barriers to Degree Completion" at Morgan. This report and internal process took on several iterations as other self-studies were introduced with greater priority such as our Middle States Accreditation Self-Study, the Foundations of Excellence in the First College Year Self-Study, and the Baldrige Criteria Self-Study, among others.

The Barriers to Degree Completion report became buried in my "to-do" list. Whenever a new associate provost came on board and became my supervisor (I'm on my fourth supervisor since I've been in the position), I would inform them about these identified barriers and show them corresponding evidence to support the significance of their impact. With each change in leadership, perhaps one of these identified barriers would move up on the list of priorities at the institution.

As the years progressed, I continued to update this report with new evidence and more current examples of how these barriers were affecting our retention and graduation rates. When Dr. David Wilson became president of Morgan State University in 2010, he invited division and department heads to present to him and his cabinet an overview to include a historical context for the division or department, successes, challenges, and proposed solutions. I was ready!

Finally, my Barriers to the Degree Completion report would have an audience of senior administrators at the institution. I had amassed the data, I had outlined the examples, and I had spent years simplifying and truncating the information into what some may call "an elevator speech." The barriers were: (1) money (paying for college); (2) degree requirements; (3) policies and procedures; (4) customer service; (5) technology; (6) academics and academic advising; and (7) campus culture. Tackling these barriers has contributed to our increase in retention and graduation rates at the university.

New leadership often affords new opportunities to present ideas and innovations, but will you be ready? A side note: One change that President Wilson made that challenged us in the best of ways was his request that we shorten our annual reports that sometimes had consisted of countless pages, even bound volumes of words, to not more than two pages annually. This single directive has resulted in more concise, targeted, and strategic communication from his subordinates. All of our points still are made effectively, and President Wilson is free to request additional information at his discretion.

## THE FUTURE OF THE HBCU PRESIDENCY

Today's HBCU presidency requires the president to have a personality and gift for raising money for the university while he maintains the traditional connection to faculty and students. A president is required to keep his finger on the pulse of the university's lifeline of recruitment, retention, and graduation rates, as well as changing technology, including online education (Hayes, 2013).

A 2014 survey of HBCU college presidents, which identifies seven pressing priorities for HBCUs, concludes that the ability to effectively communicate to students and their families the value of an HBCU education is the primary and critical issue for the future of HBCUs (AGB, 2014).

Freeman and Gasman (2014) have observed a recycling of presidents at HBCUs and found that although grooming of future presidents is taking place, it does not appear to be systematic. Many presidents interviewed for the Association of Governing Boards of Universities and Colleges study pointed to the lack of a presidential pipeline, especially in the development of the quality of leadership required to meet the challenges of the future. "Gone are the days of decades of top-down leadership, now replaced by a need for charismatic personalities who are well-skilled at fundraising while navigating internal needs and external stakeholders, as well as politics and long-standing traditions" (Hayes, 2013).

## CHAPTER 1: QUESTIONS AND NEXT STEPS

1. Do you understand the leadership style of the president of your institution and its potential benefits to the institution?
2. Identify institutional leadership challenges and think through proposed solutions.
3. Are proposals and recommendations with supporting data ready for presentation to the president without notice?
4. Align the retention, completion, and student success strategies of the institution with the leadership style and strategic priorities of the institution's president.
5. Is a member of the student success and college completion team at the institution involved in the selection process for a new president?
6. Provide talking points and data benchmarks for the institution's president so that the student success accomplishments (and challenges) remain in the forefront of the president's agenda.
7. Follow the president on social media and track the public position statements, blogs, editorials, and commentaries of the president.

# REFERENCES

AGB. (2014). *Top Strategic Issues Facing HBCUs, Now and into the Future.* A Report by the Association of Governing Boards of Universities and Colleges. Available at http://agb.org/reports/2014/top-strategic-issues-facing-hbcus-now-and-future.

Carnegie Corporation (2013). *Carnegie Corporation of New York Honors Higher Education Innovators with 2013 Academic Leadership Award: Presidents of Arizona State, Duke, Spellman and Stanford Win Grants.* Press release, December 9, 2013. Available at http://carnegie.org/news/press-releases/story/view/carnegie-corporation-of-new-york-honors-higher-education-innovators-with-2013-academic-leadership-aw.

Collinson, D. (2005). Dialectics of Leadership. *Human relations, 58*(11), 1419–442.

Cook, B. J. (2012). The American College President Study: Key Findings and Take-aways. *Presidency, 15*(2). Available at www.acenet.edu/the-presidency/columns-and-features/Pages/The-American-College-President-Study.aspx.

Davis, J. (2014). Spelman College President Tatum to Retire Next June. *Atlanta Journal-Constitution*, July 9. Available at www.ajc.com/news/news/local-education/spelman-president-tatum-to-retire-next-june/ngcHH.

Freeman Jr., S., & Gasman, M. (2014). The Characteristics of Historically Black College and University Presidents and Their Role in Grooming the Next Generation of Leaders. *Teachers College Record, 116*, 1–34.

Fullan, M., & Scott, G. (2009). *Turnaround Leadership for Higher Education.* San Francisco: Jossey-Bass.

Gasman, M. (2012). What Presidents Can Learn From Walter Kimbrough. *Chronicle of Higher Education*, May 30. Available at http://chronicle.com/blogs/innovations/what-presidents-can-learn-from-walter-kimbrough/32631.

Gasman, M. (2013). *The Changing Face of Historically Black Colleges and Universities.* Philadelphia: Center for Minority Serving Institutions, University of Pennsylvania.

Gasman, M., Baez, B., Drezner, N. D., Sedgwick, K. V., Tudico, C., & Schmid, J. M. (2007). Historically Black Colleges and Universities: Recent Trends. *Academe*, 69–77.

Hayes, D. (2013). HBCU's Presidents at a New Crossroad. *Louisiana Weekly*, December 23. Available at www.louisianaweekly.com/hbcus-presidents-at-a-new-crossroad.

Howard, G. (2012). Michael Sorrell Revived Paul Quinn College (and Almost Died Doing It). *Dallas Observer*, February 16, 2012. Available at www.dallasobserver.com/2012-02-16/news/michael-sorrell-revived-paul-quinn-college-and-almost-died-doing-it/2.

Keierleber, M. (2014). Hampton U. President Helps Raise Its Minimum Wage with a Personal Gift. *Chronicle of Higher Education*, January 23. Available at http://chronicle.com/blogs/bottomline/hampton-u-president-helps-raise-its-minimum-wage-with-a-personal-gift.

Kimbrough, W. (2011). Black Colleges Still Play a Vital Role in Education. *Chronicle of Higher Education.* Available at http://chronicle.com/article/article-content/128038.

Lipinski, J. (2014). Norman Francis to Retire after 46 Years as Xavier University President. *NOLA.com, The Times-Picayune*, September 4. Available at www.nola.com/education/index.ssf/2014/09/norman_francis_to_retire_after.html.

Rovaris, D. J. (2005). *Mays and Morehouse: How Benjamin E. Mays Developed Morehouse College, 1940–1967.* Silver Spring, MD: Beckham Publications.

Taylor, J., & Machado, M. D. L. (2006). Higher Education Leadership and Management: From Conflict to Interdependence through Strategic Planning. *Tertiary Education and Management, 12*(2), 137–60.

Tierney, W. G. (1988). Organizational Culture in Higher Education: Defining the Essentials. *Journal of Higher Education*, 2–21.

## Chapter Two

# Branding

## *Understanding What Makes Your University Great and Putting It Out There*

The word *brand* is defined as a kind or variety of something distinguished by some distinctive characteristic; a kind, grade, or make as indicated by a stamp, trademark, or the like; to stigmatize, to impress indelibly, to label or to promote. *Corporate branding* is defined as an attempt to attach higher credibility to a new product by associating it with a well-established company name. A corporate brand will potentially have a rich heritage, assets and capabilities, people, values and priorities, a local or global frame of reference, citizenship programs, and a performance record (Aaker, 2004).

Colorado State University (CSU) defines the word *brand* as a set of expectations that stakeholders associate with the university and its services. This university further states that at the core of every brand is a pledge to those you serve—a promise to consistently do or offer something in a way that they have come to expect. CSU believes that in building the brand, consistency is key, and each time constituents come in contact with CSU, they naturally form and reshape their opinions of Colorado State University.

In this chapter, the word *brand* is used to understand what makes an institution great and how to communicate it to the community at large. Contrary to popular belief, all HBCUs are not the same. Every institution has a uniqueness—characteristics and identity that distinguish the institution from all others. Yet, unfortunately, perception often becomes reality. HBCUs frequently are lumped together by mass media and portrayed as inferior or substandard based on the challenges that many HBCUs face. All institutions have a brand; has the brand been assigned by mass media, by common perceptions, or by the institution itself?

13

*Chapter Two*

## BRANDING BY MASS MEDIA

Headlines such as "Fighting for Survival," "HBCUs That Have Closed Their Doors," "HBCU Closures: A Reversible Trend?" and "Is There a War on HB-CUs?" appear in publications such as *Diverse: Issues in Higher Education*, *Inside Higher Ed*, and *Essence* magazine and can become an HBCU's brand, especially if individual institutions do little to counteract public perception. "This normalizing of turmoil across HBCUs is supported by the underrepresentation of HBCU stories in the media and national education publications. The low levels of mainstream coverage received by these institutions allow for single stories to be held as representative of all HBCUs" (Stroud, 2014, p. 11).

Stroud discusses the ways that media perceptions of HBCUs have assisted in the production of stories and generalizations that many times have presented HBCUs in monolithic terms (p. 25). Moreover, the diversity of mission, purpose, and programs at HBCUs should be celebrated and emphasized as institutions move forward with brand cultivation. A 2014 report by the Association of Governing Boards of Universities and Colleges—*Top Strategic Issues Facing HBCUs, Now and into the Future*—quantifies that:

> marketing and branding—the ability to effectively communicate to students the value of an HBCU education—were cited by many (college) presidents throughout the survey and during the focus group as key strategic issues that influence the overall value of HBCUs and, inevitably, impact enrollment. . . . Many institutions are grappling with how to re-envision the historic mission of the HBCU brand for the 21st-century student. They are writing a new story to convey the uniqueness of their mission and program offerings. Many others are concerned with changing the overall public perception of HBCUs and are devising strategies to highlight how HBCUs greatly contribute to regional workforce needs. (pp. 2–3)

## WHAT IS YOUR BRAND?

In 2005, Morgan State University participated in the Foundations of Excellence in the First College Year Self-Study. Dr. John Gardner, president of the John N. Gardner Institute for Excellence in Undergraduate Education and founder of the Foundations of Excellence program, visited Morgan's campus and served as keynote speaker for one of our annual faculty institutes.

He spoke that day about the value of the institution's brand, especially for first-year students and their parents. He presented his observations and perceptions of the Morehouse College brand. He talked about how everyone knows (or at least perceives) that Morehouse men don't use profanity, don't smoke, dress in business casual attire, and know how to tie a bow tie. He reminded us that students and parents expect Morehouse to hold to the standards of the "Morehouse Mystique" by expecting the young men at Morehouse to be well-spoken, articulate, and comfortable in leadership roles.

He highlighted the success of some private HBCUs (Morehouse College, Spelman College, Hampton University, and Howard University) in creating well-recognized "household name" brands and mottos. He challenged the audience of faculty, staff, and administrators at Morgan State University to think seriously about what the Morgan State University brand is. How is that brand communicated to first-year students and their parents, both before they arrive at Morgan, and once they are enrolled?

I left the Faculty Institute that day motivated to think about how I perceived the Morgan State University brand and how the brand was being communicated to our new students and their parents.

## DEVELOPMENT OF A BRAND

Medina and Duffy (1998) identify "five main brand positioning dimensions: a university's learning environment (including excellent staff, facilities and resources); reputations (including brand name, achievements and high standard of education); graduate career prospects (including graduates' employment prospects, expected income and employers' views of graduates); destination image (including political stability, safety and hospitality) and cultural integration (including religious freedom and cultural diversity)" (Hemsley-Brown & Oplatka, 2006, p. 331).

One author proposed strategies to help institutions of higher education better position themselves in the minds of their targets, first by measuring their current positions, and second by presenting possible approaches to changing their positions. The author cautions higher education professionals to remember that an institution's goal is not merely to attract the best students to attend the first day of classes, but rather to retain those students through graduation and beyond as loyal alumni (Herr, 2001).

## PERCEPTION: THE HBCU RENAISSANCE

In recent years, thanks to new movies and syndicated reruns on many cable networks, movies such as *Drumline* and *Stomp the Yard*, as well as television shows such as *A Different World*, HBCUs have made their way into the pop culture narrative of today's college-age students. These fictitious portrayals and plotlines depict HBCUs from the most positive of perspectives—predominantly black institutions where diverse students excel in music, pledge fraternities, participate in sacred rituals and traditions, enjoy meaningful friendships, and make their families proud after persevering to earn their degree(s). This HBCU portrayal excites students and parents alike, especially when institutions incorporate these positive perceptions into brand messaging.

## TO BE AN HBCU OR NOT
## TO BE AN HBCU—THAT IS THE QUESTION

A few years before President David Wilson arrived at Morgan State University, there were discussions about expanding the university's image beyond that of just an HBCU. There were conversations about removing historically black fraternity and sorority plots and outdoor seating areas from our overall campus landscaping design, as well as using more diverse photographs and messaging in our print materials.

While we all agreed that diversity was very important on our campus, there were some apprehensions about moving away from our roots by removing historic symbolism and landmarks from the campus. Without prompting, I decided to begin collecting data about why students choose to apply to Morgan, and why students choose to enroll at Morgan once they have been accepted to the institution.

I began to use a brief survey embedded in the Accuplacer test to ask freshmen these questions providing all of the possible answers that had been discussed in the meetings that I had attended during months of engaging dialogue on the subjects of diversity and the campus environment. Students are asked, "What influenced you the MOST in making your decision to ENROLL at Morgan State University?" with the following possible responses:

- My parent(s) encouraged me to enroll at Morgan.
- I wanted to continue a family tradition of Morgan alumni.
- I wanted to attend an HBCU.

- Morgan offered me the best financial-aid package.
- I was offered an Honors scholarship.
- I was impressed by the reputation of the academic programs.
- I attended a fall and/or spring Open House program.
- Morgan was affordable.
- I like Morgan's location.
- I was impressed by the appearance of Morgan's campus and facilities.
- My friends or classmates attend or will be attending Morgan.

Students are permitted to select only one of the aforementioned responses. For every year, beginning in 2008, with a sample of size of 750–1,250 freshmen each year, the number one response is always "I wanted to attend an HBCU." This data bears witness to the power of the HBCU brand and its allure to prospective and new students at Morgan State University. This data undergirds our decision in 2008 to completely rebrand the new-student orientation program for first-time freshmen with an increased emphasis on HBCU legacy and tradition, with specific emphasis on the Morgan State University brand.

Our new students are not choosing Morgan in spite of the fact that we are an HBCU, but rather *because* we are an HBCU; our new-student orientation brand at Morgan State University embraces and reinforces a proud HBCU brand while still promoting and developing diversity.

## LET DATA INFORM THE BRAND

Chapter 3 discusses the power of data and how understanding the students at an institution of higher education and their characteristics should drive strategic student retention programs and initiatives. When it comes to branding a college or university, data should inform the brand. Because all HBCUs are not the same, institutional data should be used to provide insight into who prospective, current, and former students are and what attracted them to an institution and/or what drove them away from an institution.

At Morgan, more than 75 percent of the new students every year are still first-time freshmen straight out of high school, primarily age 18. At many institutions, the composition of the new student body each year has shifted to include more mature students, transfer students, part-time students, and returning (stopped-out) students. According to the National Student Clearinghouse, 38 percent of all postsecondary students in a fall term are adult learners twenty-five years of age or older (Newbaker, 2012). This underscores the importance of understanding the profile of the student population of an individual institution before cultivating the brand.

Branding for HBCUs is not "one size fits all"; it's individual and unique; and data should inform the development of a brand that will appeal to the targeted student population at the institution. What will be impressive and informative to an eighteen-year-old who lives on campus as a full-time student and his/her parents is very different from what will be impressive and informative to a part-time, returning student of age 46 who works full time. Understanding the strengths of the institution and aligning those strengths with the profile of the targeted student population will produce the best and most unique brand for the institution.

## REBRANDING NEW STUDENT ORIENTATION

Beginning in 2008, the Office of Student Success and Retention (OSSR) at Morgan State University assumed leadership over the new-student orientation program for first-time, full-time freshmen. Orientation at Morgan is a four-day experience that begins on Sunday and ends on Wednesday of each week with a new group of students and parents attending every week. The branding for this program is twofold: the Morgan State University brand and the branding of students as a graduating class from the very beginning.

The Morgan State University brand during new-student orientation is focused on legacy, tradition, alumni, and excellence. From the start, students are taught the significance and relevance of HBCUs throughout U.S. history, in general terms, and Morgan's historical significance throughout U.S. history in more specific terms. (See appendix B, "Notable Morgan State University Alumni.")

The orientation highlights the achievements of outstanding alumni, introduces students to Morgan traditions and rituals including the school spirit song, the university's special line dance, school spirit chants, and what it means to become a "Morgan man" or a "Morgan woman." The university's brand is outlined, and institutional expectations are communicated. Students and parents are receptive, energized, and impressed.

The second level of branding throughout the new-student orientation experience at Morgan occurs at the student level by branding new students from the beginning of their matriculation as the graduating "Class of. . . ." New incoming freshman students in 2015 became known as the graduating "Class of 2019." This brand is communicated and reinforced on T-shirts, backpacks, and even with a graduation tassel that is given to every student during the opening program of new-student orientation by the president himself, Dr. David Wilson.

This brand assignment, the "Class of . . . ," plants the seed from the very first day a student steps on campus that the expectation, and the commitment, is that every student can and will graduate in four years. The president of the university gives a special "charge" to new students and parents during the opening program that lays a foundation that is built on throughout the orientation program. Graduation in four years is a goal supported by the institution and its staff, faculty, and administrators.

## BRAND COHESION: ALIGNMENT WITH STRATEGIC GOALS OF THE INSTITUTION

President David Wilson brought with him in 2010 a new motto for Morgan State University: "Growing the Future, Leading the World." This new brand motto would serve as a foundation for a new strategic plan, revised vision statement, core values, and mission for the institution. The strategic goals of the institution are: Enhancing Student Success, Enhancing Morgan's Status as a Doctoral Research University, Improving and Sustaining Morgan's Infrastructure and Operational Processes, Growing Morgan's Resources, and Engaging with the Community. The core values for the institution are excellence, integrity, respect, diversity, innovation, and leadership.

Any and all branding should be consistent with the mission, vision, strategic goals, and core values of the institution (Smith, 2013). The OSSR at Morgan has labored to ensure that the brand messaging of its programs and initiatives are consistent with and supportive of these goals and values.

## "PUTTING IT OUT THERE": COMMUNICATING THE BRAND

A brand is more than just a logo, motto, or slogan. Thus, communicating the brand takes more than just the visualization or imprinting of the brand logo. Institutions can communicate the brand through print materials, social media, common and universal talking points for faculty, staff, and administrators, as well as the institution's website.

Oregon State University (OSU) outlines the brand identity of the institution on the institution's website including the "brand personality," core messages, and points of pride (http://oregonstate.edu/brand/home). OSU has brand-identity guidelines inclusive of their brand statement: "Oregon State University is an authentic community, whose accomplishments, inclusive excellence, innovation and leadership promote a healthy planet, wellness and economic progress."

Similarly, the Ohio State University has a website for the institution's brand that includes the history of the brand, the basis of the brand, and the brand personality. The basis of the Ohio State brand includes this statement: "The Ohio State brand is rooted in our history, our identity, and our achievements, all of which are inextricably linked to our core mission: To advance the well-being of the people of Ohio and the global community through the creation and dissemination of knowledge. Our brand looks to the future, too, ready for tomorrow's challenges and opportunities" (http://brand.osu.edu). Ohio State University has been successful in establishing a well-known brand and reputation as a public research university that is consistently well rated, well ranked, and well reviewed.

## "WE ARE THE BEARS!"

The Morgan State University school spirit song is "We Are the Bears" and asks the question, "Who Are We?" Every institution, particularly HBCUs, must ask the question, "Who are we?" An institution cannot afford to take for granted or to assume that common perceptions or the "word of mouth" reputation of the university is consistent with the brand. Once the institution has answered the question of who they are and what makes the institution great and unique, consistently communicating the brand both on and off campus is paramount.

Ultimately, there is a connection between the brand image of the institution and student expectations, student retention, and student success; when a student perceives a favorable brand, and the matriculation experience "lives up" to favorable perceptions, the likelihood of student retention increases (Belanger, Mount & Wilson, 2002).

## CHAPTER 2: QUESTIONS AND NEXT STEPS

1. Does the institution have a corporate-style brand inclusive of a logo, motto, brand identity, and core values?
2. Is the institution's brand consistent with the vision, mission, and strategic goals of the institution?
3. Survey current students to collect data about their perceptions of the institution including why they chose to apply, enroll, and remain at the institution.
4. Survey former students, both alumni and no-longer-enrolled students, to capture their perceptions including their retrospective reflections of the institution's brand image.

5. How is the institution's brand communicated to prospective students, current students, and alumni?

6. Develop a strategy to incorporate the institution's brand into key student success initiatives such as new-student orientation, freshman seminar classes, parent workshops and weekends, university events, and convocations.

7. Provide talking points, data, and updated facts to campus stakeholders (faculty, staff, administrators, alumni, community partners) so that the brand of the institution is well-known, easily articulated, supported by current data and facts, readily available, and consistent.

## REFERENCES

Aaker, D. A. (2004). Leveraging the Corporate Brand. *California management review*, *46*(3), 6–18.

AGB. (2014). *Top Strategic Issues Facing HBCUs, Now and into the Future.* A Report by the Association of Governing Boards of Universities and Colleges. Available at http://agb.org/reports/2014/top-strategic-issues-facing-hbcus-now-and-future.

Belanger, C., Mount, J., & Wilson, M. (2002). Institutional Image and Retention. *Tertiary Education and Management*, *8*(3), 217–30.

Hemsley-Brown, J., & Oplatka, I. (2006). Universities in a Competitive Global Marketplace: A Systematic Review of the Literature on Higher Education Marketing. *International Journal of Public Sector Management*, *19*(4), 316–38.

Herr, P. (2001). Higher Education Institutional Brand Value in Transition: Measurement and Management Issues. In M. Devlin (Ed.), *Forum Futures 2001: Exploring the Future of Higher Education* (pp. 23–26). Cambridge, MA: Forum for the Future of Higher Education.

Medina, J. F., & Duffy, M. F. (1998). Standardization vs Globalization: A New Perspective of Brand Strategies. *Journal of Product & Brand Management*, *7*(3), 223–43.

Newbaker, P. (2012). More Than One-Third of College Students Are Over 25. *National Student Clearinghouse.*

Smith, R. D. (2013). *Strategic Planning for Public Relations.* New York: Routledge.

Stroud, Q. (2014). Black Colleges, Media, and the Power of Storytelling. In F. Commodore (Ed.), *Opportunities and Challenges at Historically Black Colleges and Universities* (pp. 11–26). New York: Palgrave Macmillan.

*Chapter Three*

# Data Mining

## *Who Are Your Students, and What Do They Need?*

Data mining, big data, data analytics, and descriptive and predictive analytics all have emerged as "buzzwords" and hot topics in higher education. Just about every conference, summit, and symposium in higher education includes some level of data and predictive analytics in its subject matter.

Data-driven decision making and strategic planning are the byproducts of this new culture of evidence, accountability, and outcomes in higher education. The underlying concept of this new data culture is to motivate institutions to evolve beyond just reporting data and transition into data-driven and evidence-based decision making and predictive modeling.

Educause, the association of information-technology leaders and professionals committed to advancing higher education, defines *analytics* as "the use of data, statistical analysis, and explanatory and predictive models to gain insights and act on complex issues" (Bichsel, 2012, p. 6). According to one author, "Big data is a generic term that assumes that the information or database systems used as the main storage facility are capable of storing large quantities of data longitudinally and down to very specific transactions. . . . This information can be used by institutional researchers to study patterns of student performance over time, usually from one semester to another or from one year to another" (Picciano, 2012, p. 12).

In 2002, Luan defined *data mining* as "the purpose of uncovering hidden trends and patterns and making accuracy based predictions through higher levels of analytical sophistication" (p. 19). In the context of this chapter, data mining is simply using data to better understand who your students are and what they need. At HBCUs, this is a critical and often oversimplified question, the question of who students really are and what the institution should be doing to meet their needs. If answered correctly, student retention, progression, degree completion, and overall success can be fostered and promoted at HBCUs.

A 2014 report published by the Education Trust examining the top ten analyses at eight institutions to provoke discussion and action on college completion observes that these high-performing and fast-gaining institutions "typically had a self-described 'data geek' in a key leadership role whose own curiosity about what the data might say about various aspects of student success started the ball rolling" (Yeado, Haycock, Johnstone & Chaplot, 2014). The genesis of good data mining is just getting underway; someone on campus must get the ball rolling.

## WHO ARE THE STUDENTS
## AT MORGAN STATE UNIVERSITY?

Morgan has an enrollment of approximately 7,500 students, with approximately 6,300 undergraduate students. More than 95 percent of Morgan undergraduates receive some type of financial aid and more than 55 percent are Pell eligible. Morgan State University still is primarily a first-time, full-time population of African-American students, about 70 percent of whom are first-generation college students. More than 65 percent of undergraduate students at Morgan test into developmental English, reading, and mathematics courses. By every traditional measure and predictor in higher education, many Morgan students are "high-risk" students.

Several years ago, Morgan State University conducted two studies to investigate the issue of (then) declining retention and graduation rates: (1) "Predicting Initial Success and Retention: Querying a Longitudinal Cohort Database"; and (2) "Predicting Graduation Rates for the Four Year Public Colleges in Maryland: An Analysis of the Education Trust Data 2003–2006 and Implications." Both studies were authored by the director of institutional research (IR) and a senior faculty member in the Department of Psychology.

Their findings are as follows: In the first study, first-year retention was used as the dependent variable in a binary logistic regression using gender, high school GPA, SAT verbal and SAT math scores, unmet need as a percentage of cost of attendance, and fall GPA as predictors of first-year retention. The study found that where unmet financial need was greater than or equal to 70 percent, attrition from the freshman to sophomore year was significantly higher. There was no significant association between retention rates and gender, SAT verbal and SAT math scores, or fall GPA at Morgan State University.

In the second study, a multiple regression analysis was used to predict graduation rates for four-year public colleges in Maryland using Pell grant status, mean SAT scores, percent underrepresented minorities, and dollars spent per FTE (full-time enrolled student). The study found that correlations among Pell status, SAT scores, and underrepresented minorities were substantial. Further, the percentage of Pell grant recipients was the most significant predictor of six-year graduation rates. The higher the percentage of Pell recipients on a campus, the lower the retention and graduation rates were for that campus.

Additionally, Morgan's Office of Institutional Research studied 2009–2010 attrition data and discovered the following: (1) first-semester academic success was an excellent predictor of first- to second-year retention; (2) students from outside of Maryland were less likely to return for a second year than Maryland residents; and (3) Pell grant recipients were less likely to be retained than non-Pell recipients.

Each of these studies revealed the very significant relationship between finance and funding for college and retention and graduation rates at Morgan State University. As Morgan students continued to struggle with the economic crisis (2008–2012 especially), the recession and recovery, and their percentage of unmet financial need each semester, Morgan's retention and graduation rates continued to suffer in correlation to their finances. Through data mining, predictive analytics, and the use of big data, Morgan State University continues to investigate the factors associated with retention and graduation rates in an effort to identify and address causes of student attrition.

## TRUST THE DATA; DON'T "SECOND-GUESS" THE DATA

Following several years of declining retention rates after the year 2000 (our retention rate had been in the low seventies for more than a decade until it dropped into the sixties for the 2001 cohort of freshmen), our university began an introspection and critical analysis of our admission policies. At that time, *selectivity* and *college access* were still buzzwords in higher education. Colleges and universities were being urged to "build" their incoming freshman class based on predictive models for success to include SAT and high school GPA as predictors.

Our IR team already had begun to observe correlations between our students' ability to pay their tuition and fees each semester and/or students' unmet financial need and their likelihood to return the following term and to persist over time. Despite the mounting evidence that our students' financial circumstances were the number one factor associated with our attrition, some voices at the institution rang loudly that our admission criteria was too liberal.

These voices brought data, both national and statewide, to the table to suggest that our retention and graduation rates would increase if we simply became more selective in our admission process. Administrators, faculty, and staff engaged in months of spirited debate over the idea of increasing our minimum SAT/ACT and/or GPA requirements. Our director of admission, at the time, was opposed to such an increase, as was I, based on the understanding that financing college and paying the bill were our primary issue.

Well, despite our supporting data and mounting evidence that selectivity would not increase our retention and graduation rates, a decision was made at the executive level to increase our admission criteria for the fall 2005 incoming freshman class. A snowball effect of negative consequences resulted from this epic decision. First, our freshman class was reduced from 1,337 students in fall 2004, our highest number of first-time, full-time freshmen in history, to only 765 freshmen in fall 2005.

The voices behind the decision argued that we would make up our enrollment deficit based on an increase in retention and graduation rates for this cohort over time. The retention rate for the fall 2005 cohort of 765 students was 66.9 percent and the six-year graduation rate was 28.9 percent, our lowest graduation rate in the history of the institution. While this freshman cohort had our highest SAT and GPA average in history, because of the fact that they did not have greater financial means to pay their bills, we suffered a 50 percent loss in first-time freshman enrollment and historic declines in retention and graduation.

The moral of the story is: don't second-guess the data! Even when national and statewide trends may be pointing in a different direction, trust the data analytics and data mining on your campus.

## WHERE'S THE DATA?

Every institution should make transparent and functional data available to the student retention, success, and support team. Data such as retention and graduation rates, household income, SAT/ACT profiles, high school GPA, term-by-term progression, and remediation rates, as well as gateway course and faculty data, transfer-student profiles, data by program, major, college, and school, and data by race and ethnicity, gender and age, part-time and full-time status, and in-state and out-of-state residency are baseline metrics for the beginnings of data analytics and data mining for student success and retention.

Colleges are required to report much of this data to state and federal agencies through the Integrated Postsecondary Education Data System (IPEDS). Accrediting agencies such as the Middle States Commission on Higher Education and the Southern Association of Colleges and Schools Commission on Colleges mandate detailed data reporting and analysis by colleges and universities. Additionally, external funding grantors, both private and public, require detailed data reporting. On individual campuses data can be obtained from students' admission application, the Free Application for Federal Student Aid (FAFSA), and the college's Student Information System.

On every campus there are pockets of "small" data, sometimes in silos, with data custodians who need only to be approached and asked for permission to access their data. Offices such as career development, alumni affairs, academic departments and schools, athletics, residence life and housing, Title III, the first-year experience, and other offices and departments own small pieces of data that may never have been integrated into the larger data spectrum on the campus.

Standardized national assessments of student learning are an important component of Morgan's Comprehensive Assessment Plan. Six national assessments have been used to measure the student experience at Morgan: the National Survey of Student Engagement, the Cooperative Institutional Research Program Freshman Survey, the Collegiate Learning Assessment (CLA), the Measure of Academic Progress and Proficiency, the iSkills Information Literacy Assessment, and the ETS major field tests in business, biology, and chemistry. The greatest challenge to the success of these initiatives is usually student participation.

Response rates and participation rates for several of these assessments have been low, and there is an ongoing effort to identify motivational factors and incentives that will help increase student response rates. At Morgan, additional data is collected through the Accuplacer placement examination. Also, Morgan administers an exit survey to graduating seniors and a follow-up survey to graduates of the institution, and annual student-satisfaction and parent-satisfaction surveys are conducted in an effort to improve customer service and promote quality control.


## WHAT IS THE COLLEGIATE LEARNING ASSESSMENT?

The CLA is an innovative approach to assessing an institution's contribution to student learning and the "value added" by the institution. The CLA measures are designed to simulate complex, ambiguous situations that every successful college graduate may face in the future. Life is not like a multiple-choice test, with four or five simple choices for every problem; thus, students are asked to analyze complex material and provide written responses. CLA measures are uniquely designed to test for critical thinking, analytic reasoning, written communication, and problem solving, skills that most academicians agree should be the outcomes of a college education (Shermis, 2008).

As a CLA participant, Morgan State University first assessed the institution cross-sectionally, testing a sample of first-year students in fall 2005 and a sample of seniors in spring 2006. Implications of the 2005–2006 CLA results at Morgan were that although freshmen performed below the expected level, seniors performed at the expected level.

The initial value-added score was higher than expected for the university. Although the 2005 cohort of freshmen performed below expected, when compared to seniors in the spring of 2006, results demonstrated that the university was providing a substantial contribution or overall "value added" to student learning outcomes. From year to year, CLA results vary at the institution providing fresh and ongoing insights into freshman preparedness and the value added by the institution once students arrive on campus.

## WHAT DATA COMES FROM ACCUPLACER?

The purpose of Accuplacer is to provide useful information about students' academic skills in mathematics, English, and reading (www.accuplacer.collegeboard.org). The results of the assessment are used by academic advisors to determine students' course placement. Accuplacer is an adaptive test. Questions are chosen on the basis of students' answers to previous questions. This technique selects just the right questions for students' ability level. At Morgan, all first-time freshmen (except transfer, CASA Academy, and NEXUS students) are required to take the Accuplacer placement test.

With an average of 65 percent of students testing into one or more developmental courses, results are consistent with national data; Accuplacer results are consistent with the previous ETS and Accuplacer placement test results at Morgan, although rates of developmental courses are increasing. Results confirm the CLA data, proving again that students are less prepared than expected. Accuplacer results indicate that at least two-thirds of first-time freshmen need development or "remediation," and only a handful of students pass the diagnostic tests in the developmental courses administered during the first week of classes.

The Accuplacer placement test provides the university with a level of individual student adaptability, systematic accuracy, and administrative flexibility in an effort to appropriately place new students in freshman courses consistent with their level of preparation and skill. For the past eight years, the OSSR has used the Accuplacer test to survey first-time freshmen about their first-generation college status, their decision to apply to Morgan, their decision to enroll at Morgan, their access to technology, and their financial need. Survey questions from the institution can be embedded into the Accuplacer placement test allowing for data collection from the majority of incoming freshmen each year. This data has revealed significant trends and consistency across academic years.

## USE DATA TO ANSWER QUESTIONS

When considering student retention, student success, and degree completion, there are always questions. These questions include: How effective is remediation at the institution? Why are students leaving? Why did students choose to attend this college in the first place? Is new-student orientation working? Where do students go when they leave? Who are the best faculty on campus? What are the barriers to degree completion? The answers to all of these questions can be found through data mining and data analytics.

One concern on many college campuses is why and how these questions garner differing answers though data analysis. A response to this concern is simply: how was the question asked, by whom was the question asked, and for what purpose(s) was the question asked? The IR office should serve as the official data repository, warehousing all official data for the institution. Thus, all data analysis should be vetted by the institutional research team.

A simple question such as "What is our graduation rate?" can be misinterpreted and answered in a variety of ways depending on how the question is asked, by whom the question is asked and for what purpose(s), and who provides the answer to the question.

The IPEDS definition of a graduation rate is the percentage of a first-time, full-time, fall freshman cohort that has completed their degree at the end of six consecutive years at the same institution. This rate does not include transfer students, part-time students, and students who begin in any term other than fall (Horn, 2006).

Unfortunately, the clock does not stop for a student who "stops out" or withdraws for a semester or a year during the six years of matriculation allotted by IPEDS. On a college campus where faculty and staff may be reporting four-year, five-year, and/or six-year graduation rates for various programs, subpopulations, and grants, different people will have different versions of a "graduation rate" for the institution. All of the various graduation rates may have some validity depending on the purpose for reporting a specific version of a graduation rate.

Be cautious of working outside of collaboration with the IR team at an institution. "Apples to apples," and "oranges to oranges" comparisons are crucial to data mining and predictive analytics. "Apples to oranges" data mining at an institution can have a domino effect of negative consequences and implications. The OSSR at Morgan State University works closely with the Office of Institutional Research to answer the hard questions and meet the data and reporting requirements of external agencies and grantors, as well as the strategic goals of the OSSR.

## DATA AND STRATEGIC RETENTION GOALS

Recognizing that retention research is important, exploring not only an individual's personal journey from admission to graduation, but also the university's ongoing commitment to each student's success, the OSSR at Morgan State University established an overall retention goal to systematically collect and make available data regarding student retention for the purposes of reporting, assessment, and evaluation. It was intended that any data gathering, examination, and reporting would result in identifying factors that describe, explain, and predict student retention (and attrition) at Morgan State University.

Working in collaboration with various campus programs and departments, the OSSR works to: develop for its own use standardized formats for reporting information, gathering data, and documenting that priority-area goals are being attained; use available data to highlight priority areas where goals are being met successfully as well as areas where improvement may be needed; develop methods for gathering data and information to support the encompassing work of the OSSR; develop research projects to examine the impact of related activities on student retention; collaborate with all campus departments and programs to ensure that retention goals and objectives are being met; and better understand the campus-wide implications of retention program goals and objectives.

OSSR strategies to implement a consistent system of data collection and evaluation include:

- *Attrition Rates*—Each semester continuing students who are not registered for classes are contacted by retention staff in order to determine their status

at the university. Students who withdraw from the university officially are
contacted and asked to complete an exit survey.

- *Tracking Persisters*—Systematic study of students who persevere through
  to graduation is required to determine commonalities and consistencies in
  course of study, major fields of interest, extracurricular activities, etc. . . . in
  an effort to establish a core of "best practices" for students from matriculation to graduation. Results of the study of persisters have implications for
  university requirements, policies, and procedures.
- *Student Surveys*—Student-satisfaction surveys are an example of how
  students can provide important information regarding customer service,
  university-to-student communication, campus resources, etc. . . . Entrance
  and exit surveys are utilized for new students and graduating students to
  answer a myriad of questions regarding student success and retention.
- *Retention Rates*—Six-year retention rates are systematically calculated and
  maintained within each department in every school, and are updated in a
  centralized database within the Office of Institutional Research. The OSSR
  works in conjunction with IR to present and preserve accurate university-
  wide retention data.

## DATA-DRIVEN DECISION MAKING

The emphasis at state and federal levels on increasing retention and graduation rates and the inevitability of performance-based funding have incentiv-
ized self-imposed, data-driven decision making at Morgan. The potential
negative impact of low graduation rates on any public HBCU's funding and
reputation, especially when graduation rates are analyzed without context for
the unique student populations served at HBCUs, can serve as a motivating
factor for senior leadership to make data-driven decisions.

When the OSSR submitted a report in conjunction with a Barriers to Degree Completion Taskforce documenting that Morgan required more credits-
to-degree in many majors than other public universities in Maryland such as
Towson State University, the University of Maryland–Baltimore County, and
the University of Maryland–College Park, who require only 120 credits for
most majors, a decision to cut all degree programs to 120 credits (with the
exception of several specific program-accredited majors) resulted.

For example, the following credit-hour requirements were in place: dance
education major (157 credits), engineering major (133 credits plus 4–11
prerequisite math credits before MATH 241), biology major (127 credits),
computer science major (134 credits), nursing major (134 credits), architecture major (126 credits), construction-management major (131 credits),

information systems major (127 credits), and accounting major–CPA track (127 credits)—all required credits in excess and above 120 credit hours not including required developmental (remedial) courses. In 2012, the Maryland Higher Education Commission reported that Morgan graduates had the highest number of earned credits at public universities in the state of Maryland, averaging 138 hours at the time of completion (more than fifteen credits above the state average).

Morgan State University has participated in various self-studies including the Middle States Accreditation Self-Study, the Baldrige Criteria Self-Study, Foundations of Excellence, Noel-Levitz, Six Sigma, and an internal Comprehensive Process Review resulting in recommendations and changes as indicated by the results of the self-study or analysis. These changes include the addition of a university call center to help handle high call volume, a revamped General Education Core, updates to outdated academic policies, developmental course redesign, the phasing out of university-wide exit writing and speech proficiency examinations for graduating seniors, and the implementation of a first-year advising model using professional advising staff from the OSSR and Center for Academic Success and Achievement.

Romero and Ventura suggest that data mining is the best way for college administrators to evaluate and organize institutional resources, both human and material, and educational offerings. The authors further suggest that data mining, in general, enables data-driven decision making for improving current educational practices and learning materials at an institution. It is recommended that educators and institutions develop a data-driven culture that guides decision making (Romero & Ventura, 2013).

## SO WHAT DO YOUR STUDENTS NEED?

Morgan State University students need financial support! Every data analysis bears out the challenges that Morgan students face in meeting their financial obligations every semester. Not only do Morgan State University students need direct financial support, but also they need support in navigating the financial-aid process. Morgan's data-driven approach to student success has led to an intrusive approach to obtaining student financial support including FAFSA filing campaigns, a financial-literacy program, enhanced need-based institution aid and service requirements, and a one-on-one "case-management" style financial clearance and reinstatement process every semester.

The data at the institution should dictate the institutional priorities to enhance student success, retention, and degree completion. This is the fundamental framework for data mining and predictive analytics. Every institution is unique; determining who your students are and what they need should be driven solely by data and evidence, not by anecdotes or popular trends.

## WRITE THE DATA NARRATIVE
## FOR YOUR OWN INSTITUTION

In Maryland, the chance of receiving a baccalaureate degree by age 24 is only 8 percent for the lowest household-income quartile of $36,100 or less (Organisation for Economic Co-operation and Development, 2012). The chance of receiving a baccalaureate degree by age 24 in Maryland is 17 percent for the second-lowest income quartile of $36,100–$65,300; it's 36 percent for the second-highest income quartile of $65,300–$108,300. However, for the highest income quartile in Maryland with a household income of $108,300 or above the chance of receiving a baccalaureate degree by age 24 is 82 percent. The majority of students at Morgan fall into the lowest two income quartiles representing low-income families.

This data is rarely shared in any articles published by the Baltimore press or in a report to the Maryland legislature. Instead, citizens of Maryland are led to believe that the four public HBCUs are inferior based on low retention and graduation rates, especially compared to the flagship public institutions such as the University of Maryland–College Park or the University of Maryland–Baltimore County. However, when retention and graduation rates are reported in conjunction with the household income profile of students at the institution, obvious direct correlations are prevalent. Institutions must take the lead in letting data tell the student success story both on and off campus. Taking leadership in writing the data narrative for the institution can result in changes on campus as well as changes in perceptions and policy off campus.

## CHAPTER 3: QUESTIONS AND NEXT STEPS

1. Has the institution participated in self-studies, and how were the results used to promote a culture of data-driven, evidence-based decision making?
2. Take inventory of existing national survey and assessment data on campus to determine what national databases are available for data mining.
3. Identify the data custodians on campus and request permission to access their data for the purpose of fostering student success.
4. Are student success and retention administrators involved and/or included in data-driven decision making at the institution?

5. List all of the metrics used to identify institutional priorities associated with improving retention and graduation rates.
6. Initiate a partnership with the Office of Institutional Research to include the development of data-driven strategic retention, persistence, and completion goals.
7. Make a list of questions pertaining to student success, attrition, and persistence, and assign these questions to specific data sets and analysis models to pursue the answers.

## REFERENCES

Bichsel, J. (2012). *Analytics in Higher Education: Benefits, Barriers, Progress, and Recommendations.* Louisville, CO: EDUCAUSE Center for Applied Research.

Horn, L. (2006). Placing College Graduation Rates in Context: How 4-Year College Graduation Rates Vary with Selectivity and the Size of Low-Income Enrollment (NCES 2007-161). Postsecondary Education Descriptive Analysis Report. National Center for Education Statistics. Washington, DC: U.S. Government Printing Office.

Johnson, L., Adams, S., Cummins, M., Estrada, V., Freeman, A., & Ludgate, H. (2013). *The NMC Horizon Report: 2013 Higher Education Edition.* Austin, TX: New Media Consortium; EDUCAUSE Learning Initiative.

Luan, J. (2002). Data Mining and Its Applications in Higher Education. *New Directions for Institutional Research, 2002*(113), 17–36.

Organisation for Economic Co-operation and Development (2012). Education at a Glance 2012: OECD Indicators. OECD Publishing. Available at www.jec.senate. gov/public/?a=Files.Serve&File_id=04a5e372-05d5-4f06-a95e-ede43027c6cd.

Picciano, A. G. (2012). The Evolution of Big Data and Learning Analytics in American Higher Education. *Journal of Asynchronous Learning Networks, 16*(3), 9–20.

Romero, C., & Ventura, S. (2013). Data Mining in Education. *Wiley Interdisciplinary Reviews: Data Mining and Knowledge Discovery, 3*(1), 12–27.

Shermis, M. D. (2008). The Collegiate Learning Assessment: A Critical Perspective. *Assessment Update, 20*(2), 10–12.

Van Barneveld, A., Arnold, K. E., & Campbell, J. P. (2012). Analytics in Higher Education: Establishing a Common Language. *EDUCAUSE Learning Initiative, 1,* 1–11.

Yeado, J., Haycock, K., Johnstone, R., & Chaplot, P. (2014). *Learning from High-Performing and Fast-Gaining Institutions: Top 10 Analyses to Provoke Discussion and Action on College Completion.* Washington, DC: The Education Trust.

## Chapter Four

# Frontloading

## Freshmen, First
## Impressions, and Foundations

Much has been documented in higher education about the importance of the first year in the retention and graduation of undergraduate students. Dr. Vincent Tinto (1993), a pioneer in student retention research and theory, identifies the following four institutional actions that enhance retention and graduation rates:

1. providing support (e.g., tutoring, developmental courses, study groups, summer bridge programs, academic advising freshman seminar, etc.);
2. connecting academic support to everyday learning (e.g., supplemental instruction, linked courses, etc.);
3. effective assessment (e.g., entry assessment, early warning systems, student learning, student engagement, advising, teaching, etc.);
4. engaging students on learning (e.g., learning communities, collaborative teaching strategies).

Noel-Levitz, Inc. (2007), one of the nation's leading higher education resources, has identified the following causes of student attrition: adjustment/transition difficulties, academic difficulty, uncertainty of educational/career plan, congruence/fit (e.g., boredom, dissonance, irrelevance, isolation), finances, goal change or attainment, and extra-institutional factors.

The first year of college is the time to "hit the ground running" and prevent students from becoming bored, feeling isolated, or simply not adjusting to the transition from high school to college. The classic cliché still holds true: "You never get a second chance for a first impression." All of Vincent Tinto's best practices should come into focus immediately during the critical first year of college.

## FOUNDATIONS

As one of the four public HBCUs in Maryland, Morgan State University's Access and Success Program has been funded by the state of Maryland with oversight from the Maryland Higher Education Commission (MHEC) since 1999. The purpose of the Access and Success Program in the state of Maryland is to provide the public HBCUs with dedicated funding to improve retention and graduation rates in an effort to help close the achievement gap for college students in Maryland.

Initially, four Access and Success goals were outlined by Morgan State University: (1) to enhance tutoring programs; (2) to enhance educational programs in residence halls; (3) to strengthen advising programs and enhance monitoring of student progress; and (4) to create a program for first-time freshmen.

After years of documented success rates for student participants in specific initiatives such as the Access-Success Summer Bridge Program, the PACE (Pre-Accelerated Curriculum in Engineering) Program, the Academic Enrichment Program, and other programs funded by Maryland's Access and Success grant for HBCUs, Morgan State University decided to expand these initiatives and move to a campus-wide student success model for all students with an emphasis on orientation, transition, and the first year of college. This decision was consistent with Kuh, Cruce, Shoup, Kinzie, and Gonyea's 2008 conclusion that:

> because students generally benefit most from early interventions and sustained attention at key transition points, faculty and staff should clarify institutional values and expectations early and often to prospective and matriculating students. To do this effectively, a school must first understand who its students are, what they are prepared to do academically, and what they expect of the institution and themselves. (p. 555)

In October of 2003, Morgan State University expanded the original goals of the MHEC Access and Success Program for student retention and graduation by reorganizing its campus retention program from a highly centralized model with a specific emphasis on its summer bridge program cohorts to a model that is coordinated centrally but with the focus on resources and accountability shifted to the major academic units. Thus, the Office of Student Retention (now known as the OSSR) was created in the fall of 2003 in the division of Academic Affairs. The first cohort of students to enroll under this campus-wide retention model was the fall 2004 cohort of first-time freshmen.

## FRONTLOADING

In an effort to "frontload" critical resources and provide a strong foundation for new freshmen, Morgan State University implemented the following documented best practices in student retention research and theory with the goal of increasing student retention and six-year graduation rates:

- Summer Programs—Incoming freshmen are encouraged to participate in a six-week summer program the summer before their first semester of matriculation in an effort to facilitate a smooth transition from high school to college. Students are presented with an opportunity to receive additional academic preparation in the areas of English, reading, and mathematics. (Summer programs have included the Access-Success Summer Bridge Program, CASA Academy, ACCESS Orientation, PACE, etc.)
- Academic Advisement—Students are required to meet with their academic advisor at least once per semester. Departmental faculty advisement is supplemented by mandatory first-year advising with the CASA and the OSSR staff serving as the first-year advisors.
- Tutoring—Students are encouraged to utilize tutoring services for all four credit classes and classes in which students experience difficulty. Tutoring is provided by the Center for Academic Success and Achievement (CASA), the Academic Enrichment Program (AEP), the schools within the university, and by organized peer groups.

A 2004 ACT report, *What Works in Student Retention? Four-Year Public Colleges*, cites several retention practices at high-performing (retention and degree completion) four-year public colleges that differentiate those colleges from low-performing colleges such as:

> advising interventions with selected student populations, increased advising staff, comprehensive learning assistance center/lab, integration of advising with first-year programs, a center that combines academic advising with career/life planning, summer bridge program, non-credit freshman seminar/university 101, recommended course placement testing, performance contracts for students in academic difficulty, residence hall programs, and extended freshman orientation for credit. (p. 6)

## SUMMER ORIENTATION—BEGIN AT THE BEGINNING

One of the new retention initiatives for the 2008–2009 academic year was the ACCESS Orientation Program. During the new ACCESS Orientation

Program, students and their parents receive financial-aid assistance including FAFSA information, residence-life information, placement-testing results, academic advisement, and career counseling. Additionally, students participate in activities, workshops, and seminars that include topics such as college transition, school spirit, study skills, and test-taking strategies. Morgan State University recognizes that the freshman year is a challenge for all new students. Completion of this program has served as a first step toward success for Morgan's new college students.

New college freshmen and their parents leave the ACCESS Orientation Program week with all of the necessary tools and resources required for their enrollment at the university, as well as for their first year of academic success. Morgan offers four (or five depending on enrollment) four-day ACCESS Orientation Program sessions for a maximum of 250 students per session in order to accommodate at least one thousand to twelve hundred first-time freshmen during the months of July and August.

The OSSR hires twenty-six peer mentors to work with the incoming first-time freshmen during each week of freshman orientation. Higher education research has long supported the benefits of peer mentoring to include increased academic performance and higher retention (Terrion & Leonard, 2007).

In fact, Bean and Eaton (2001) suggest that "mentors become a vehicle for adaptation to and integration into a student's academic and social communities . . . and for students who are avoidant, mentoring may be the best method of intrusion . . . making a student more likely to become active in adapting to the environment" (p. 84).

Findings of one study suggest that even a short-term freshman-orientation experience may positively influence student persistence (Pascarella, Terenzini & Wolfle, 1986). The authors of the study further suggest that rather than a one-time experience of limited duration prior to student enrollment, orientation to college may be more effective as an ongoing enhancement to student success integrated into the campus academic and social systems throughout the first year of college.

The ACCESS Orientation Program at Morgan has increased access to college for a diverse student population, prepared students for their college matriculation, provided a head start for students on the path to academic success, and helped to increase the retention and graduation rates of all undergraduate students by means of "frontloading" critical resources for first-time, full-time freshmen. The new and revamped campus-wide ACCESS Orientation Program for freshmen and new students imbued with the best practices in higher education has yielded outstanding results for the entire undergraduate student population.

# HBCU ORIENTATION: A CULTURAL TRANSITION MODEL

When new-student orientation at Morgan was moved from the Counseling Center to the OSSR in 2008, an opportunity to completely reconsider, reshape, and revamp the existing orientation program for new students presented itself. For several years, I had worked with the orientation program as coordinator of the academic components of the program, placement testing, and academic advisement. I knew that I wanted to reshape the way that we advised students in the summer and also transition from paper-and-pencil placement testing to a robust, adaptive, computer-based placement test (Accuplacer).

Meanwhile, there had been significant discussion in upper-management team meetings about why students choose to attend Morgan. When we transitioned to Accuplacer, I began to collect data via a survey embedded in the placement exam to provide answers to why students chose to apply to Morgan and why they decided to enroll at Morgan.

Consistently, the number one answers for each year that I have posed these questions (every year beginning in 2008) to more than eight hundred freshmen annually has been that students chose to apply because "I visited the campus" and students enrolled because "I wanted to attend an HBCU." This data about students' desire to be a part of the HBCU campus culture, one that they may have seen in-person, perhaps on a campus visit, started me to think about what I call "the HBCU Renaissance."

Movies and television shows such as *Stomp the Yard*, *Drumline*, *School Daze*, *The Great Debaters*, and *A Different World* have captivated a new generation of young African-Americans. These young people come to our HBCUs eager to experience the culture that they have already been exposed to through the imagery of movies and television.

The second reason our students identify in terms of why they chose Morgan State University is that a family member or someone that they know attended Morgan. With this data in hand, we decided to embrace the rich culture of our HBCU from the start by incorporating a cultural transition theme throughout our orientation program.

We begin with a "shock and awe" opening program that showcases the best of our university including our world-renowned choir, marching band, the president, senior administrators, and peer mentors. We highlight the outstanding accomplishments of the institution such as the number of three- and four-star African-American generals produced by our Army ROTC program, which is second only to West Point in the number of African-American generals produced, the number of Fulbright study-abroad scholars that our institution produces, which is highest among all HBCUs, the numerous awards that the university has won, grants received, and accreditations earned, and we "shout out" our many distinguished and notable alumni who have accomplished great things in their respective fields, many of whom are well-known celebrities.

The next three days of the four-day orientation program include students watching the movie *The Great Debaters*, an HBCU alumni panel that discusses "Why HBCUs?: Legacy and Leadership," a special Morgan's Got Talent night that features the new, incoming freshmen in the program, and an authentic Rites of Passage closing ceremony created and conducted by one of our senior faculty in the Department of Sociology and Anthropology.

During the closing ceremony students are asked to reflect on their daily experiences in freshman orientation, both cultural and academic, and then they are required to write a statement of affirmation and purpose. Students are invited to come to the podium, one-by-one, and share their statements of affirmation with their new peer group and be affirmed by their new graduating class.

Every year, during each week of the orientation program, faculty and staff listen as new students express how much their perspective has changed and improved in such a short period of time. The most impactful event during the orientation always is the trip to the National Great Blacks in Wax Museum located in Baltimore. Student after student comments that even though so many people may have doubted their potential along the way including some family, educators, and even a few friends, when they observed the perseverance and resilience of people of color in the United States over generations through the images at the museum and listened to their stories as told by the docents and griots, they affirmed their newfound belief and confidence in their own potential as well as the privilege that they have been afforded to attend college.

Even our non-African-American students comment about the impact of their experience at the National Great Blacks in Wax Museum, stating how much they learned and how welcomed they felt by their new peers in this new HBCU experience.

The second most popular event during the orientation experience is the Morgan Spirit 101 session. This session began later in the orientation program when President David Wilson, who arrived on campus in 2010, mentioned to me that he was missing students' enthusiastic school spirit that he had observed at universities such as Auburn University, where students went "all out" at games and pep rallies to show their school spirit.

In 2011 we added the Morgan Spirit 101 session to the program; at this time our awesome peer mentors engage new students in the traditions of our campus by teaching them Morgan's chants, cheers, songs, and even our university line dance to our theme song, "We Are the Bears." As a result, we've seen our students become more and more enthusiastic at games and pep rallies. It was just as simple as showing students how to demonstrate their spirit from the beginning so that they wouldn't have to wait to observe our traditions over time before participating in them.

Although it is tempting for HBCUs with often-limited financial resources to limit new-student orientation to one day or reduce the experience to simply placement testing and advisement only, our cultural transition model at Morgan produces a solid foundation for freshmen who are primarily eighteen-year-old students of color who need a well-rounded approach to college transition with structured, in-person support that acknowledges their desire to participate in the "HBCU Renaissance" on our campus.

## GOALS AND OBJECTIVES OF SUMMER ORIENTATION

The goals of the ACCESS Orientation Program are:

1. to introduce new students and parents to Morgan State University (more than 70 percent of first-time, full-time freshmen are first-generation college students);
2. to provide new students with a strong foundation for academic success through placement, advisement, workshops, and seminars that cover note-taking strategies, test-taking tips, and study skills;
3. to facilitate the required transactions for enrollment with the offices of financial aid, the bursar, the registrar, health services, and residence life;

4. to help transition students from high school to college in a positive, safe, and controlled environment;
5. to promote relationships among new students and their peers, as well as with faculty, staff, and administrators;
6. to make students and parents aware of the many resources available to undergraduate students including the CASA, the OSSR, the AEP, the Career Development Center, the Counseling Center, and the Student Government Association.

The desired outcomes for this flagship orientation program at Morgan are:

1. new students and parents will have their decision to enroll at Morgan State University affirmed, supported, and celebrated by faculty, staff, and administrators;
2. new students and parents will become familiar with the campus and become familiar with the campus environment;
3. new students will receive quality academic advisement;
4. new students will be taught note-taking strategies, test-taking tips, and study skills;
5. new students will learn strategies for time management, stress management, and conflict resolution;
6. new students and parents will complete the enrollment process before August 1st including submitting their health forms, providing their final high school transcript, filing for financial aid, applying for housing, registering for classes, paying their balances due, and receiving their Morgan ID card;
7. new students and parents will make lasting connections with other new students and parents, peer mentors and upperclassmen, and key staff and administrators.

The ultimate goals of the ACCESS Orientation Program initiatives are to build and shape the freshman class, to increase freshman-sophomore retention rates, and to increase persistence to graduation for all undergraduate students. The academic, cultural, and practical components of the ACCESS Orientation Program foster the fulfillment of these goals. In addition to evaluating the program by using weekly parent and student evaluations for each event within the orientation program, a general survey to measure the impact of orientation as perceived by students and parents is administered. To take program evaluation to the next level, it became important to analyze the ACCESS Orientation Program through a broader lens by benchmarking survey results with peer institutions.

# MEASURING SUCCESS: STUDENT ORIENTATION OUTCOMES BENCHMARK STUDY

The Student Orientation Outcomes Benchmark Survey is administered every two years approximately one to three months following ACCESS Orientation (by the end of November) in an effort to evaluate the effectiveness of the freshman-orientation program at Morgan State University and to compare the results at Morgan to the results at thirty to fifty other institutions of higher learning.

Results of the Student Orientation Outcomes Benchmark Survey are housed by the NASPA Assessment & Knowledge Consortium (www.naspa consortium.org), a collection of assessment instruments focused on key areas within Student Affairs. NASPA consortium studies are designed to provide colleges and universities with actionable campus-specific and benchmarking data to shape and enhance programming inside and outside the classroom.

The OSSR has participated in the Campus Labs (formerly known as Student Voice) Student Orientation Outcomes Benchmark Study in 2010, 2012, and 2014 to evaluate the effectiveness of the ACCESS Orientation Program new-student orientation "cultural transition" model; for three consecutive evaluations, Morgan State University students rated the ACCESS Orientation Program significantly better than students rated their orientation program at the thirty-plus benchmark institutions for twenty-six of the forty-five measurable outcomes.

# CASA ACADEMY—A MODEL PROGRAM

Higher education research has long identified the summer bridge program as an effective strategy for improving student success (Walpole et al., 2008; Habley & McClanahan, 2004; Gold, Deming & Stone, 1992; Garcia, 1991). The CASA Academy program at Morgan State University is a six-week summer bridge program offered by the Center for Academic Success and Achievement that serves as an alternative admissions program for high school graduates who did not meet the SAT/ACT and/or GPA criteria used for regularly admitted students.

The CASA Academy program is designed to ease the transition from high school to college for students whose academic profile and performance suggest the need for early intervention to improve their potential for success in college. Approximately three hundred students are enrolled in CASA Academy and are required to pass the following three remedial courses with no grade lower than a "C": Developmental Mathematics, Developmental Reading, and English.

The CASA Academy provides six to eight weeks of coursework, tutoring, mentoring, academic advisement, and college-transition workshops for the two hundred–plus participants. There is no cost to students who are residents of the state of Maryland for tuition, fees, room and board, meals, or books. If successful, these students are admitted to Morgan and can move on to the university's Freshman Studies Program. Morgan has observed improvement in the CASA Academy students' success in terms of their first-year GPAs and earned credits. The addition of the *StrengthsQuest* curriculum and teaching methodology to the CASA Academy Program can be credited for improving success rates of cohorts of CASA students since fall 2010.

## THE QUEST FOR STRENGTHSQUEST

In 2010, the director of the Center for Academic Success introduced Strengths-Quest to the winning CASA Academy model. StrengthsQuest is an online instrument published by Gallup that identifies five signature themes of talent that can be developed into strengths with thirty-four possible themes. StrengthsQuest is used by over 4 million people in seventeen languages (more than 200,000 college students). Strengths-based training models have been linked with positive outcomes for student retention (Swanson, 2006) and leadership development (Lehnert, 2009). Through the CASA Academy strengths-based orientation seminar, taught by the CASA advising staff, students learn that their overall academic experience can be greatly enhanced by the perspective and direction they take in setting goals and making key decisions.

Strengths-based advising helps students learn ways of capitalizing on their strengths in order to succeed. A strengths-based approach starts with the assumption that by becoming more aware of their own strengths, students are motivated to set goals, achieve at a higher level, make better choices, and complete tasks. Advising sessions shift students' focus from problems to possibilities. Several studies have reported that students randomly assigned to a strengths-based advising approach as first-year students are significantly more satisfied with their advising experience than are students with advisors who used traditional academic advising models (Gallup, 2012).

## SIX WEEKS OF "MATH BOOT CAMP"

In a 2000 report published by the Educational Resources Information Center in *ERIC Digest*, "Summer Bridge Programs: Supporting All Students," it is noted that many institutions offer more than one summer bridge program, accommodating the unique needs of their student population, and that individualization of summer programs for a campus is critical.

At Morgan, a second six-week summer bridge program, the Pre-Accelerated Curriculum in Engineering (PACE) Program, has achieved outstanding results. In addition to support received through external grant funding, the OSSR has invested up to $75,000 per fiscal year in the PACE Program.

The goal of the six-week PACE program is to prepare first-time freshmen majoring in engineering (civil, industrial, and electrical engineering) for the placement examination in mathematics. Students take classes in mathematics, computer science, English composition, physics, and chemistry. Also, students participate in a research rotation and science fair.

The fifty students who participate in the PACE program every summer have an 80 percent chance of testing into MATH 241 (Calculus) at the end of the program. PACE students are six times more likely than non-PACE freshmen to test out of Developmental Math (MATH 106). Participation in the PACE Program significantly increases students' rate of persistence to graduation.

## FOUNDATIONS OF EXCELLENCE®
## IN THE FIRST COLLEGE YEAR

In 2005, Morgan State University was one of fourteen colleges and universities invited by the Policy Center on the First Year of College to participate in a self-study, the Foundations of Excellence® project, designed to help institutions of higher education evaluate and improve the overall experience of first-year students. The year-long study utilized a well-developed model of excellence for the first college year.

The purpose of the Foundations of Excellence® is to encourage colleges and universities to engage in a comprehensive process that acknowledges both institutional strengths and needs for improvement related to the first year. As Morgan State University systematically evaluated its level of achievement within each of nine dimensions, it simultaneously identified those areas in which an actionable change in policy or practice could yield improvement in institutional intentionality, efficiencies, student learning, and retention. The institution prioritized desired changes in an implementation plan for campus improvement, a strategic working document that could guide Morgan's present and future approach to the first year.

The centerpiece of the Foundations of Excellence is a model for first-year excellence comprised of a set of principles that are termed Foundational Dimensions®: Organization, Improvement, Diversity, Faculty, Transitions, Roles and Purposes, All Students, Learning, and Philosophy. The engine of the process is a campus-based task force—a group with broad representation from across campus.

The work of the task force begins with a campus audit of the first year (Current Practices Inventory), continues with a year-long process using the dimensions and related performance indicators, and culminates in an action plan for campus improvement. Active participation by faculty members fostered the achievement of even higher levels of success.

The Foundations process is a collaborative process among faculty, staff members, students, and administrators. The process relies on multiple sources of evidence, both quantitative and qualitative, as well as involvement of many campus participants who lend their perspectives and professional judgment to rethinking the first year. The self-study and improvement-planning portions of the Foundations process are designed to be completed in one calendar year.

## FIRST-YEAR ADVISING

The goals of academic advising are: (1) to engage students in learning; (2) to promote students' academic success; (3) to foster students' personal and intellectual growth; and (4) to assist students in carrying these goals into their roles as citizens and lifelong learners (NACADA, 2005). One of the most consistent trends traceable through all ACT surveys of academic advising is the growth in the percentage of institutions reporting the existence of a professional academic advising center/office—from 30 percent in 1983 to 73 percent in 2004 (Habley, 2004).

A "shared" or "complementary" advising model consists of both professional and faculty advisors. Students at Morgan State University are advised by professional academic advisors (CASA and OSSR staff) for their first year, and then they are assigned faculty advisors at the beginning of their second year who advise them until their subsequent graduation from the university. Possibly the most challenging task for new students is creating a course (class) schedule. In an effort to circumvent the frustrations of schedule-making for new students, blocked course scheduling of freshman courses was created by the Office of Records and Registration to ensure course availability and schedule cohesion.

First-time freshmen are advised by the OSSR staff according to their school or by the CASA staff in small groups during their designated AC-CESS Orientation Program week. Academic holds are placed on the student accounts of all first-time freshmen that require them to speak with their first-year advisor before they register for classes, make any changes to their course schedule, or drop a class.

The assigned first-year academic coaches and mentors initiate contact with students throughout the semester. Additionally, students are encouraged to sign up for the alumni mentors and the adopt-a-freshman programs during their first year. Unfortunately, even with periodic phone calls and ongoing email communication to first-year students, some students still do not respond to multiple outreach efforts.

## TUTORING AND COLLABORATIONS

Another best-practice strategy for first-year success, consistent over many years of study, is peer tutoring, which has been shown to increase all levels of student learning (Annis, 1983). Every semester at Morgan, the OSSR provides structured peer tutoring in each of the academic colleges/schools of the university. All freshmen are encouraged to take advantage of peer tutoring via the Center for Academic Success and Achievement (CASA), the Academic Enrichment Program (AEP), or tutoring provided in the various academic units as available. There is no charge for access to peer tutoring or for any campus tutoring program.

The Office of Residence Life (ORL) has been in partnership with the OSSR and has received funding from the OSSR in the past to support retention efforts in the residence halls. The OSSR provided funding to purchase new computers for ten computer labs located in the various residence halls. Also, the ORL offers the AEP, a program designed to increase retention and graduation rates by offering tutoring, workshops, and interventions for students who live in the residence halls. Also, the ORL is piloting a living-learning communities program in which students are assigned housing based on their major fields of study.

The AEP is a residentially based student academic support initiative directed by the ORL. The program provides comprehensive services that are designed to help students from all majors and classifications achieve their academic goals by offering opportunities for individual growth and development. The program strives to meet students where they are by providing them with an opportunity to have a seamless transition into college and promoting an educational experience that does not end when students leave the classroom.

## DON'T FORGET THE PARENTS

Harper, Sax & Wolf (2012) suggest that institutions "support the need for parent orientations that provide guidance on the college transition . . . (and that) parents engage their students in more frequent discussions about course-taking and academic progress, at least during the first year of college" (p. 151).

A critical component of summer orientation at Morgan State University each year is the Parents' 411 parent-orientation program. This program is conducted in conjunction with the ACCESS Orientation Program. During this one-day orientation, parents work in groups and identify their top three concerns. Consistently, campus safety, academics, and money emerge as the top three concerns of parents.

In an effort to address parent concerns on a continual basis, the OSSR publishes a parent newsletter that is mailed by hard copy to parents of undergraduate students at least once per academic year. Each parent newsletter highlights a specific area of focus at the university such as student retention, campus safety, study abroad, academic development, disability support services, advisement, Foundations of Excellence in the First College Year, etc. Also, parents are reminded of upcoming dates and deadlines for students such as registration, FAFSA renewal, and the last day to drop classes. The goal of the *Parents' 411* newsletter is to inform parents and family members (who may not be Morgan alumni) of the great programs and positive initiatives offered at Morgan and to affirm students' decision to attend Morgan State University.

## COLLEGE GPS: THE FRESHMAN-ORIENTATION COURSE

There is a positive correlation between the completion of a freshman-orientation course and academic performance and retention; students who complete an orientation course in their freshman year often have higher GPAs and are more likely to have returned for a second year.

At Morgan, the freshman-orientation course introduces students to the expectations and demands of higher education, to the legacy and tradition of Morgan State University, to college survival strategies, and to the broad array of career opportunities in their major field of study. The course is designed to act as a map for students by charting their path from matriculation to graduation. The freshman-orientation course curriculum includes an increased emphasis on maintaining financial aid and funding for college, as well as helping freshmen to understand budgeting and debt.

The orientation course engages active participation of various student-support services in class lectures and assignments. Participants are the CASA, the Counseling Center, the Academic Enrichment Program, the offices of financial aid, residence life, and student activities, and the Career Development Center. Eight weeks of the orientation course focus on overall student success at Morgan and eight weeks focus on how to be successful in students' specific college/school and major field of interest.


## WHAT FOLLOWS THE FIRST YEAR

The first college year is central to the achievement of an institution's mission and lays the foundation on which undergraduate education is built (Alexander & Gardner, 2009). The sophomore year serves as a year of transition for undergraduate students as they progress toward their goal of graduation. The "sophomore slump," a term that refers to the tendency of students to do worse academically in their second (sophomore) year than in their first (freshman) year, can be avoided by extending the same level of support from the freshman year through the sophomore year (Wilder, 1993).


## THE FINAL IMPRESSION OF FIRST IMPRESSIONS

Each specific retention initiative at Morgan State University is evaluated annually based on cohort participation. For example, student participants in the CASA Academy summer bridge program have higher retention and graduation rates and higher GPAs than their peers with similar admission profiles who do not participate. PACE students are six times more likely to test out of developmental mathematics than their peers who do not participate.

Specific measures are used on an annual basis to evaluate every program and initiative sponsored by the OSSR. The results indicate that when students participate in targeted first-year programs and retention initiatives, they earn higher GPAs and have higher retention and graduation rates.

Thus far, Morgan's greatest achievements at the campus-wide level for the first-year college experience have been the introduction of the ACCESS Orientation Program for all first-time, full-time freshmen, participation in the Student Orientation Outcomes Benchmark Study, the ongoing enhancement of six-week summer bridge programs such as the CASA Academy and PACE Program, the publication of the *Parents' 411* newsletter and development of the Parents' 411 parent orientation and workshop, the implementation of professional academic advisement in the first year, and the integration of first-year services under the Enrollment Management and Student Academic Support Services (EMSASS) division fostering seamless support for first-year students.

Consistent with the EMSASS integration at Morgan is Tinto's (2003) statement that "successful institution retention programs are the result of the coordination across the campus of a variety of different types of programs, academic and social, that seek, in differing ways, to integrate and support students and promote their becoming effective learners while in college" (p. 9). At Morgan, maximizing the benefits of existing campus resources, improving first-year services, communicating positively with parents, and ensuring access to intrusive academic support for first-time freshmen has enhanced the delivery system of comprehensive student services and, in the final analysis, upgraded the ability of the institution to retain students.

## CHAPTER 4: QUESTIONS AND NEXT STEPS

1. Take inventory of all of the orientation, transition, and first-year programs, services, and initiatives at the institution.
2. Develop a model and framework for the first year of college to include "frontloading" best practices such as summer orientation, bridge programs, parent orientation, academic advisement, and the freshman-orientation course.
3. How does the institution evaluate and measure the effectiveness of orientation, transition, and first-year initiatives at the institution; can the results be benchmarked with data from other institutions?
4. Is the institution making the best use of peer mentoring and peer tutoring by integrating peer support throughout orientation, transition, and first-year programs?
5. Create and enforce an academic advisement plan for first-year students.
6. Engage parents by inviting their participation in workshops and activities and by communicating with them on an ongoing and routine basis.
7. Collaborate and integrate orientation, transition, and first-year initiatives with offices across divisions to include Academic Affairs, Student Affairs, Enrollment Management, and Student Success and/or Retention.

## REFERENCES

Alexander, J., & Gardner, J. (2009). Beyond Retention: A Comprehensive Approach to the First College Year. *About Campus*, May–June, 18–26.

Annis, L. F. (1983). The Processes and Effects of Peer Tutoring. *Human Learning: Journal of Practical Research & Applications*.

Bean, J., & Eaton, S. B. (2001). The Psychology Underlying Successful Retention Practices. *Journal of College Student Retention*, 3(1), 73–89.

Boudreau, C. A., & Kromrey, J. D. (1994). A Longitudinal Study of the Retention and Academic Performance of Participants in Freshmen Orientation Course. *Journal of College Student Development.*

Gallup. (2012). *Gallup Strengths Center.* Available at www.gallupstrengthscenter. com.

Garcia, P. (1991). Summer Bridge: Improving Retention Rates for Underprepared Students. *Journal of the First-Year Experience & Students in Transition, 3*(2), 91–105.

Glass Jr., J. C., & Garrett, M. S. (1995). Student Participation in a College Orientation Course, Retention, and Grade Point Average. *Community College Journal of Research and Practice, 19*(2), 117–32.

Gold, M. V., Deming, M., & Stone, K. (1992). The Bridge: A Summer Enrichment Program to Retain African-American Collegians. *Journal of The First-Year Experience & Students in Transition, 4*(2), 101–17.

Habley, W. R. (2004). *The Status of Academic Advising: Findings from the ACT Sixth National Survey.* Manhattan, KS: National Academic Advising Association.

Habley, W. R., & McClanahan, R. (2004). *What Works in Student Retention? Four-Year Public Colleges.* ACT, Inc.

Harper, C. E., Sax, L. J., & Wolf, D. S. (2012). The Role of Parents in College Students' Sociopolitical Awareness, Academic, and Social Development. *Journal of Student Affairs Research and Practice, 49*(2), 137–56.

Kezar, A. (2000). Summer Bridge Programs: Supporting All Students. Washington, DC: ERIC Clearinghouse on Higher Education.

Kuh, G. D., Cruce, T. M., Shoup, R., Kinzie, J., & Gonyea, R. M. (2008). Unmasking the Effects of Student Engagement on First-Year College Grades and Persistence. *Journal of Higher Education, 79*(5), 540–63.

Lehnert, A. B. (2009). The Influence of Strengths-Based Development on Leadership Practices among Undergraduate College Students (doctoral dissertation). Retrieved from Dissertation Abstracts International (UMI No. 3377758).

NACADA. (2005). NACADA Statement of Core Values of Academic Advising. Available at www.nacada.ksu.edu/Resources/Clearinghouse/View-Articles/Core-values-of-academic-advising.aspx.

Noel-Levitz, Inc. (2007). The Ten Most Effective Retention Strategies. Available at www.noellevitz.com.

Pascarella, E. T., Terenzini, P. T., & Wolfle, L. M. (1986). Orientation to College and Freshman Year Persistence/Withdrawal Decisions. *Journal of Higher Education,* 155–75.

Swanson, J. E. (2006). Success in the First Year: Impact of Alternative Advising on Students at a Liberal Arts College. Dissertation Abstracts International (UMI No. AAT 3246327).

Terrion, J. L., & Leonard, D. (2007). A Taxonomy of the Characteristics of Student Peer Mentors in Higher Education: Findings from a Literature Review. *Mentoring & Tutoring, 15*(2), 149–64.

Tinto, V. (1993). *Leaving College: Rethinking the Causes and Cures of Student Attrition,* 2nd edition. Chicago: University of Chicago Press.

Tinto, V. (2003). Student Success and the Building of Involving Educational Communities. *Higher Education Monograph Series, Syracuse University, 2.*

Walpole, M., Simmerman, H., Mack, C., Mills, J., Scales, M., & Albano, D. (2008). Bridge to Success: Insight into Summer Bridge Program Students' College Transition. *Journal of the First-Year Experience & Students in Transition, 20*(1), 11–30.

Wilder, J. S. (1993). The Sophomore Slump: A Complex Developmental Period That Contributes to Attrition. *College Student Affairs Journal, 12*(2), 18–27.

*Chapter Five*

# Case Management

## *Systematic Tracking and Monitoring of Students by Cohort*

Morgan State University has an enrollment just under eight thousand students, with approximately 6,500 undergraduate students. More than 95 percent of undergraduates receive some type of financial aid and more than 50 percent are Pell-eligible. Morgan State University still is primarily a first-time, full-time population of African-American students, many of whom are first-generation college students. More than 65 percent of Morgan's undergraduate students test into developmental English, reading, and mathematics courses. By every traditional measure, many Morgan State University students are "high-risk" students.

Over the past several years, Morgan changed its student success strategy for intervention with "at-risk" students from the "net approach" to the "hook approach" as the institution "fished" for students by requiring the university-wide Office of Student Success and Retention (OSSR) staff to call every "at-risk" student individually throughout each semester in order to cultivate individual relationships with students.

This single change in approach from sending mass messages, letters, and emails to students to reaching out to students by phone or by classroom visit(s) on an individual basis and tracking their responsiveness to these efforts using seamless, transparent record keeping helped to promote an increase in student retention from 67 percent for the fall 2009 cohort to 73 percent for the fall 2010 cohort; Morgan has maintained this increase for the 2011, 2012, and 2013 cohorts.

# PREDICTIVE ANALYTICS

Predictive analytics is quickly becoming one of the most popular fields in higher education. Vendors and solution providers are eager to visit institutions to offer assistance in mining data and helping to identify students on campus who are likely to succeed, as well as those students who are likely to fall by the wayside. There are several common approaches to predictive modeling in higher education.

One approach is to consider the characteristics of students at the point of initial enrollment at an institution. For example, what is the cumulative high school grade point average (GPA) of the student, what are the student's standardized test scores (SAT or ACT), what is the household income of the student, and is the student a first-generation college student? These are the most common variables factored into predictive modeling for freshman students.

Another approach, perhaps a more sophisticated model, is to use survey instruments to measure students' motivation, commitment, or "grit" as a predictive framework. Students are given an assessment to determine their personal levels of motivation, commitment, or "grit" in an effort to measure or predict the likelihood of their success in college. Duckworth, Peterson, Matthews & Kelly (2007) have found that across six studies, individual differences in "grit" accounted for significant incremental variance in success outcomes over and beyond that explained by IQ, to which it was not positively related.

A third and final approach to predictive analytics is to study the characteristics of first-year and second-year students and observe patterns that are associated with success and failure. This predictive model may identify courses, course combinations, engagement in certain campus activities, campus resources utilized, residential living style or type, and other factors that are associated with student success or failure. Denley summarizes the scope and impact of predictive analytics in a 2014 *Research & Practice in Assessment* article, "How Predictive Analytics and Choice Architecture Can Improve Student Success":

> Predictive analytic techniques move from a retrospective reporting data stance toward the use of large data sets to make detailed predictions about the future. These predictive models enable strategic action to be taken in the present to potentially provide significant improvements in the future. In this vein, an appropriately designed system could use the perspective of the past to better inform students, and conversations between students and advisors. Such a system could allow advisors and students to make plans for future semesters, illuminated by the knowledge of courses or even majors in which past students with similar programs, grades and course histories had found success. (p. 63)

The goal of these predictive models is to identify "at-risk" students at an institution. With this information, colleges and universities can target specific success and retention strategies to specific subpopulations of students. This is especially helpful at large institutions where ten thousand to forty thousand undergraduate students matriculate each year. Identifying "at-risk" students in large populations of students is critical in the delivery of student support services.

Small and midsize campuses also benefit from this information as it helps to prioritize often-limited resource delivery to the appropriate students. A 2011 article in the *Chronicle of Higher Education* cautions that "no one quite knows where education's analytics revolution will lead, but it's a safe bet that today's experiments will seem crude compared with what's coming" (Parry).

## WHY COHORTS?

As will be discussed in more detail in chapter 6, recognizing students by cohort simply means acknowledging that students are first-time, full-time freshmen who came to the institution in a fall semester or term. Students outside of a cohort are likely transfer students, part-time students, mature students, or students who came to the institution in a winter, spring, or summer semester or term. Managing the delivery of student academic support services by cohort is essential in promoting increases in retention and graduation rates!

The OSSR at Morgan requests that every student list used for the purposes of systematic tracking and monitoring includes the first-semester code and student type so that the lists can easily be sorted by cohort status. Why sort lists of students by cohort? The answer is twofold: (1) so that student-intervention efforts can be prioritized for graduating seniors, incoming freshmen, second-year students, etc.; (2) so that student-support staff always know and understand who students are and what their needs are as they endeavor to complete college in six years or less.

When students fall outside of a specific cohort, it is not that the student will not receive intervention or that the student is any less valuable to the institution, but rather resources can be designed to support the needs of the student while promoting the strategic goals of the institution at the same time.

When difficult decisions have to be made such as who gets an override in a closed course, or who should be awarded an institutional aid grant, or who should come off of the waiting list for a course that is only offered once every two years, or who should get the limited internship opportunity, or who should have their appeal to take more than eighteen credits granted, knowledge and understanding of the student's cohort designation is one critical factor for consideration in making these tough decisions.

## PREDICTING SUCCESS AT MORGAN

For many years at Morgan, the Office of Institutional Research (IR) worked tirelessly to better understand what predicts the success of Morgan students. The IR team used a number of models including logistic regression, multiple regression, cross tabs, longitudinal and retrospective trend analyses, and co-variate and multivariate models. One factor associated with student success that emerges consistently in Morgan's research is students' ability to pay their tuition and fees on time every semester.

This is consistent with the findings in a 2009 study "With Their Whole Lives Ahead of Them" published by *Public Agenda* with funding from the Bill & Melinda Gates Foundation. This study reveals that "students often bear the full responsibility of paying for school: Nearly 6 in 10 students in the study who left higher education without graduating say that they had to pay for college costs themselves, rather than being able to count on help from their families" (Johnson et al., p. 9). Further, the study found that most students leave college because they are working to support themselves and going to school at the same time.

Although more than 90 percent of Morgan students receive some type of financial aid including grants, loans, and scholarships, very few students receive 100 percent of the cost of their tuition, fees, room, board, and books. The EFC (estimated family contribution) after financial aid is awarded still presents a hardship for many students at Morgan. This difficulty is common at most HBCUs where the household income of students is significantly lower, and middle-class families struggle to make ends meet when household resources are stretched to accommodate multiple financial priorities and obligations within the household. In a 2012 editorial in the *Baltimore Sun,* Morgan's president, Dr. David Wilson, writes:

> Morgan's Office of Institutional Research conducted a study of 300-plus students who did not return and discovered that nearly 40 percent of these students were making good academic progress but simply lacked the financial resources to stay in school. If Morgan—which, in proportion to our operating budget, already contributes more institutional-based financial aid to our students than any other public university in Maryland—had the resources to award these students financial aid, our retention rate would have been comparable with retention rates at the University of Maryland College Park and University of Maryland, Baltimore County. Simply stated, lack of financial aid is a huge barrier keeping

many of Maryland's African-American students from completing their degrees within the six-year window used to determine a university's graduation rate.

## NAVIGATING THE BILL PAYMENT PROCESS

Morgan, like many other institutions of higher education, has a practice of dropping or canceling course schedules after the deadline for final payment has passed each semester. In other words, once the period for late registration/ drop and add has ended, students with outstanding balances are canceled for that semester. After a brief period is allotted for reinstatement, students must defer their registration until the following semester or for whenever funding becomes available to pay their tuition and fees.

A 2014 *Inside Higher Education* article, "Kicked Out for Nonpayment," reported that Kentucky State University had dropped a quarter of its students for failing to pay their bills and that historically students at Kentucky State had been allowed to matriculate, leave with unpaid bills, and then re-enroll without paying their bills (Rivard, 2014).

Students who are "dropped" at Morgan are less likely to have completed their Free Application for Federal Student Aid (FAFSA) on time than students who do not have their course schedules dropped or canceled. Students at Morgan who are "dropped," especially more than once, during their matriculation, have lower GPAs and lower graduation rates. Helping students to navigate the financial-aid and payment processes at the institution became a high priority with a goal of helping students to avoid being dropped or canceled, and subsequently improve their success and graduation rates.

A first step was taken to reduce the number of students who do not pay their bill on time by the Office of Financial Aid in conjunction with the OSSR. Morgan launched a FAFSA filing campaign that consisted of postcards, flyers, T-shirts, and campus announcements to promote completing the FAFSA by the March 1st deadline in Maryland. (Most states have a deadline for state grants and scholarships that is published for college students; even though the federal application is open year-round, students are ineligible for state of Maryland funding after March 1st of each year.)

A 2008 Pell Institute for the Study of Opportunity in Higher Education report, *Moving Beyond Access: College Success for Low-Income, First-Generation Students* by Engle and Tinto, reported that after six years, only 11 percent of low-income, first-generation students had earned bachelor's degrees compared to 55 percent of their more advantaged peers. This finding was due in part to lower graduation rates for low-income, first-generation students in the four-year sector where at public four-year institutions, only 34 percent of low-income, first-generation students earned bachelor's degrees in six years compared to 66 percent of their peers. The report further acknowledges the impact that unmet financial need has on the retention of low-income, first-generation students.

## THE ORIGINS OF CASE MANAGEMENT AT MORGAN

Another giant step was taken when the OSSR began to contact students about the status of their bill each semester. While the OSSR, an office housed within the division of Academic Affairs at Morgan State University, has a primary emphasis on student academic support, the influence of students' financial status at the institution cannot be denied. Initially, the director of student success and retention obtained the pre-drop list from the Bursar's Office several weeks before the deadline for final payment.

The director of the OSSR worked with the retention coordinators for each college/school to send out general letters and emails to students reminding them of the upcoming payment deadline. Then, after the deadline passed, the director of the OSSR once again obtained a list from the Bursar's Office and new letters and emails were sent to students informing them that their course schedule had been dropped along with information about the deadline for reinstatement. One major concern was preventing students from missing time in classes due to their failure to make satisfactory financial arrangements and/ or to pay their bill in full.

Over time, the Registration Committee at Morgan, a committee that has oversight over the registration process including the financial-aid and pay-ment processes and deadlines at the university, moved the drop date and the date for reinstatement back, as close to the beginning of each semester as pos-sible so that students could minimize the impact of these processes on their academic success in the classroom.

The original objective of the OSSR communication strategy for the drop was to "get the word out" to students. Later, the drop process for the OSSR evolved from a simple communication strategy to an organized case-management system that fosters seamless, transparent support for students, not only per-taining to their financial situation but also for their overall matriculation at the institution.

The "Best Practices" in Student Support Services (SSS) study (Muraskin, 1997) offered evidence of effective strategies for promoting retention for low-income, first-generation college students. The study found that SSS pro-grams with strong records of success have an active and intrusive approach to advising, seeing students more often and meeting with them several times per semester, continually tracking student performance and use of services, and checking student progress at midterm to intervene and make referrals as necessary. These programs also focus on the "whole student" in the advising process using a case-management approach.

## TO DROP OR NOT TO DROP—THAT IS THE QUESTION

Many colleges or universities simply use a hold instead of a drop to facilitate payment of an outstanding balance. When a student doesn't pay the bill or make a satisfactory financial arrangement with the bursar, a hold is placed on students' accounts preventing students from registering for courses until their obligation has been met. So once classes begin, there isn't any pressure on students to meet their financial obligation until the following semester or term. Students carry over their outstanding balance from the previous term to the next semester.

At Morgan, after a grace period expires following the deadline for final payment and/or a satisfactory financial arrangement, which may include a payment plan or deferment, student course schedules are dropped or purged from course rosters. And, after a brief period for reinstatement, students are asked to leave their classes permanently. Students are then free to re-enroll in a future term or semester without having accrued a previous balance. Because the courses and the corresponding bill for tuition and fees are purged from the system, students are eligible to re-enroll in a future term without penalty.

While the act of dismissing students from classes at a certain point early in the semester may seem harsh and punitive, at the time, it actually saves students from incurring outstanding balances beyond their capacity to pay in a given semester. Using the hold system definitely does not interrupt the delivery of course content several weeks into the semester as the drop does; however, the lack of disruption and inconvenience is short-lived.

Once students attempt to return for the next term or semester, students under the hold system often find that they have been "cut off" from the institution completely. Staff and administrators at Morgan State University continue to debate the merits of both the hold and the drop systems used to resolve outstanding balances for a population of students who struggle to pay their bill each semester.

The reality is that several hundred students at Morgan are dropped and never reinstated each semester; these are students who truly did not have the financial resources to cover their cost of attendance. Consequently, if these students had been permitted to stay in their classes without being dropped, they would have carried over their debt and been prohibited from course registration in the following semester, blocked from taking courses at any other institution of higher education, and probably sent to "Collections" to resolve the outstanding balance.

# EDUCATION ON "HOLD"

A few years ago, a young lady with whom I became acquainted through association with her parents approached me about the possibility of attending Morgan. She was thinking about attending Morgan or one of the growing and expanding private institutions in the state of Maryland. She had been a good student in high school but not at the honors or scholarship level. She was looking for general admission as a new freshman student.

After visits to both campuses, she decided that she wanted to attend the other private institution, which happened to be a very popular TWI (traditionally white institution). Knowing her parents' financial circumstances as I did, I wondered how she would be able to afford to attend this private university. When I met her the next year (she was working full-time at a deli takeout counter) and asked her about how she was doing at the other university, she informed me that she had only been enrolled there for one semester. Just as I thought, her family could not afford the expensive tuition, fees, room, and board at the institution.

Since that institution used the hold system to prevent her from registering for the following semester, she was permitted to stay in classes until the end of the first semester. She said that she didn't feel much pressure to resolve her bill, although she did know that she had a hold on her student account; everyone was just so nice to her over the sixteen-week semester until she said that she thought that eventually she would find a way to pay her bill.

When she returned for the spring semester, she found that she had been locked out of her residence hall and that she was banned from course registration. For that single semester that she matriculated at the private institution, she had accrued an outstanding bill of $16,000, and what was heartbreaking was that she asked me about attending Morgan.

I had to explain to her that without her official transcript from the private institution we would not be able to offer her admission to Morgan. Of course, without clearing her bill, she discovered that her transcript would never be released from the institution, which made her ineligible to attend any other college or university until she paid her $16,000 debt.

Under the drop system at Morgan this could never happen because this young lady would have been dropped at the beginning of the semester and would have been able to "stop out" without an outstanding balance due and simply return to Morgan when she had the funding. She would have also been free to attend any other institution.

## TRACKING AND MONITORING

OSSR staff at Morgan spend most of their time monitoring and tracking students' finances and satisfactory academic progress. OSSR staff track and systematically monitor:

- students who fail to make satisfactory payment arrangements by the deadline;
- students who fail to register for courses by the deadline;
- students who earn midterm grades of D, F, I, or W;
- students who earn final grades of D, F, I, or W;
- students who "stop-out" for one or more semesters; and
- students who have a cumulative GPA less than 2.0.

Morgan changed the strategy for intervention for these cohorts of "at-risk" students from the "net approach" to the "hook approach" requiring the university-wide OSSR staff to personally call every student on the drop list individually and to cultivate relationships with students until their final course-schedule reinstatement.

Initially using only Microsoft Excel, Oracle Application Express (APEX), and Google Docs, each semester OSSR staff track and systematically monitor students. The OSSR used APEX to identify the students, Excel to distribute the list of students assigned to each of the OSSR staff, and Google Docs to track intervention outcomes in one document made available to OSSR staff and other campus stakeholders (i.e., financial aid, bursar, academic departments).

Presently, a combination of Google Docs and Starfish Retention Solutions houses the tracking data resulting from the monitoring of these students. (Starfish is an early alert technology tool that is described in detail in chapter 7.) As students are identified who fail to make satisfactory payment arrangements by the deadline, fail to register for courses by the deadline, earn midterm or final grades of D, F, I, or W, "stop-out" for one or more semesters, or have a cumulative GPA less than 2.0, they are assigned to OSSR staff who record every outreach effort and leave notes via Google Docs and/or Starfish that detail students' specific circumstances, issues, and problems.

According to Moore and Shulock (2009), more four-year institutions are developing measures of tracking intermediate student progress to provide more points along the road to degree completion to which data can be applied to identify appropriate behaviors, strategies, and interventions for students. These milestones, benchmarks, and measures of intermediate progress are consistent with the aforementioned cohorts of "at-risk" students at Morgan.

## TRANSPARENT RECORD KEEPING

OSSR staff notes, in addition to records of any outreach efforts, are shared by giving permission to select individuals within several offices to view the information in Google Docs or Starfish. These offices may include the Office of Financial Aid, the Bursar's Office, the deans' offices, and the Office of the Provost, all of whom may access the various communications and notes pertaining to specific students over the course of the semester.

This "case-management" approach also fosters long-term relationships with students. Since the "at-risk" lists are divided up and assigned to staff according to students' major and cohort status (first-year cohort for first-time, fall freshmen), OSSR staff frequently have the same students reappearing on various "at-risk" student lists. The "at-risk" cohort lists often include students who are identified multiple times.

When OSSR staff contact students by phone or by classroom visit for one reason, the case-management approach dictates that they discuss all of the student's issues during that one intervention. Then, notes and record keeping that reflect the results of the intervention with students are posted in multiple locations in Google Docs or Starfish. In fact, the OSSR first discovered the power of this intervention style when reaching out to students on the drop list. Not only would students share their issues and concerns about their finances, but also they discussed other challenges including issues with courses, faculty, housing, their families, and so on.

## "FISHING" FOR STUDENTS

The "net approach" is simply sending out generic, mass messaging to cohorts of students within specific student subpopulations. These messages are delivered by hard copy, also known as "snail mail," or by email to students' official campus email address. For example, messages might state, "Dear Student: Our records indicate that you have an outstanding balance due for this semester." Frankly speaking, with this approach a net is cast with hopes that any student will "take the bait" and respond to the message.

The "hook approach" is sending out personal, customized messaging to cohorts of students within specific subpopulations. For example, an email may state, "Dear Tiffany: Our records indicate that you have not yet selected your classes for the upcoming semester." With this approach each student is baited individually with hopes that he or she will "bite" and respond to the message.

Currently, the approach to monitoring and tracking students at Morgan is considered to be "case management" because not only are "at-risk" students called individually and interacted with personally, but also OSSR staff continue to engage with these students who are assigned to each individual OSSR staff member on an ongoing basis and keep detailed and transparent records via Google Drive and Starfish.

## CASE MANAGEMENT: A PROVEN STRATEGY

During one recent fall semester, OSSR staff received the drop list and communicated with 2,019 students via phone calls, emails, and personalized letters. For the following spring semester, OSSR staff received the drop list and communicated with 1,221 students via phone calls, emails, and personalized letters.

Additionally, during that same spring semester the OSSR contacted: (1) students who were enrolled during either the previous spring or fall semesters and were not enrolled that spring and who had cumulative GPAs better than 2.0 (872 students); and (2) students who were enrolled during either the previous spring or fall semesters but were not enrolled that spring and had less than a 2.0 cumulative GPA (733 students). The purpose of the email communications was to invite students back to Morgan. The response was overwhelmingly positive.

In an effort to get continuing students to pre-register for fall classes, the OSSR contacted 2,251 continuing students who had not registered for that fall and invited them to meet with their academic advisors and to register for fall classes when registration reopened in that June. Again, students responded to these efforts with positive feedback.

The case-management approach has resulted in an increase in the reinstatement of students. In 2009, an average of 92 percent of students were reinstated after the drop. By 2014, almost 97 percent of students were reinstated after the drop; this increase of 5 percent is a reflection of the intrusive case-management approach to working with students to resolve their financial issues. Additionally, over time, fewer students are being dropped at the onset of a semester. The intense communication with students prior to the drop to inform them of the upcoming deadlines has helped to mitigate the numbers of students who are dropped each semester at Morgan.

## A WINNING COMBINATION

Whether it's tracking and monitoring students who fail to make satisfactory payment arrangements by the deadline, fail to register for courses by the deadline, earn midterm or final grades of D, F, I, or W, "stop-out" for one or more semesters, or have a cumulative GPA less than 2.0, the case-management approach pays substantial dividends.

Identifying "at-risk" students according to specific criteria, tracking those students by graduation cohort, reaching out to them as individuals by phone or in person, and recording the results of each intervention effort in a transparent document for other administrators to reference are winning strategies to promote student success. While different types of technology and various tools may better facilitate this case-management approach, the personal touch is what makes the difference. Hand-holding and walking students through various processes, whether they are financial or academic, yields results, results that will be reflected in the institution's retention and graduation rates.

## CHAPTER 5: QUESTIONS AND NEXT STEPS

1. Outline the profile of "at-risk" students at the institution.
2. Are predictive analytics used to better understand what predicts the success (or failure) of undergraduate students at the institution, and if so, how are the results shaping or impacting retention and graduation rates?
3. Identify students by graduation cohort within every "at-risk" student subpopulation so that student intervention efforts can be prioritized.
4. What strategy is employed to encourage students to clear their bills each semester or term, and is it effective?
5. List the specific student subpopulations that are systematically tracked and monitored by student-support staff.
6. How are the results of intervention efforts with "at-risk" students shared with the appropriate staff and administrators?
7. Develop a "case-management" approach to student success that assigns individual students to specific staff who reach out to them via personalized messaging, by phone, or in person, and record the results in transparent documents for other support staff and administrators to reference.

## REFERENCES

Denley, T. (2014). How Predictive Analytics and Choice Architecture Can Improve Student Success. *Research & Practice in Assessment*, *9*(2), 61–69.

Duckworth, A. L., Peterson, C., Matthews, M. D., & Kelly, D. R. (2007). Grit: Perseverance and Passion for Long-Term Goals. *Journal of Personality and Social Psychology*, *92*(6), 1087.

Engle, J., & Tinto, V. (2008). *Moving Beyond Access: College Success for Low-Income, First-Generation Students*. Washington, DC: Pell Institute for the Study of Opportunity in Higher Education.

Johnson, J., Rochkind, J., Ott, A. N., and DuPont, S. (2009) *With Their Whole Lives Ahead of Them: Myths and Realities about Why So Many Students Fail to Finish College*. A *Public Agenda* Report for the Bill & Melinda Gates Foundation.

Moore, C., & Shulock, N. (2009). *Student Progress toward Degree Completion: Lessons from the Research Literature*. Sacramento: California State University, Sacramento, Institute for Higher Education Leadership & Policy.

Muraskin, L. (1997). *"Best Practices" in Student Support Services: A Study of Five Exemplary Sites*. Washington, DC: U.S. Department of Education.

Parry, M. (2011). Colleges Mine Data to Tailor Students' Experience. *Chronicle of Higher Education*, December 11, 2011.

Rivard, R. (2014) Kicked Out for Nonpayment. *Inside Higher Education*, September 4, 2014.

Wilson, D. (2012). HBCUs' Success Hinges on Financial Aid: Morgan State's President Says Lack of Resources Thwarts Many African-American Students. *Baltimore Sun*, October 14.

## Chapter Six

# Strategic Initiatives

## *Programs Designed*
## *Specifically to "Move the Data"*

There has long been a debate in higher education concerning how students are "counted" for retention, graduation, and college completion. The Integrated Postsecondary Education Data System (IPEDS) for the U.S. Department of Education (www.nces.ed.gov/ipeds) mandates that all postsecondary institutions, both two-year and four-year institutions, report annually the status of students in terms of retention and graduation by first-year cohort. The students who are counted in these cohorts are limited to first-time, full-time students who begin at a two-year or four-year postsecondary institution in a fall term or semester.

This means that students who begin college in any term other than the fall term, for example, during a summer, winter, or spring term or semester, are not counted in the retention and graduation cohort data. Additionally, part-time students, transfer students, and nontraditional students are excluded from these reporting systems. In other words, only new, first-time high school graduates, typically who are age 18 at the time of their college enrollment, are counted in the assessment and analysis of college retention, graduation, and completion.

Moreover, students in the IPEDS cohort who matriculate longer than six consecutive years, or twelve consecutive semesters, count against an institution because they have matriculated beyond the cohort "cut-off" point or deadline for graduation. The Institute for Higher Education Leadership & Policy at California State University, Sacramento, suggests in their *Community College Student Outcomes: Limitations of the Integrated Postsecondary Education Data System (IPEDS) and Recommendations for Improvement* (2009) report:

> The graduation, transfer-out rates, and retention rates are the only IPEDS data that track students longitudinally. For selective four-year institutions the graduation, transfer-out, and retention rates are generally useful. Most students at

65

selective four-year universities attend for the purpose of earning a degree, attend on a full-time basis each year, enter well-prepared to succeed at college-level work, and enjoy a relatively high level of institutional resources. However, the rates are less valid for making inferences about student outcomes in less selective four-year institutions and in community colleges, especially if such outcomes are compared to those students in selective institutions. Students at less-selective institutions are less likely to attend full-time and, at community colleges, attend for a variety of purposes. At less-selective institutions, students also enter far less prepared for college-level work and most of these institutions have far fewer resources than do selective institutions. (p. 8)

## EMBRACE THE SYSTEM

While this dilemma has been discussed in previous chapters, this chapter proposes that colleges and universities, at least temporarily until IPEDS changes, embrace this system of accountability and intentionally design programs and initiatives to "move the data."

HBCUs often are associated with a supportive, encouraging, and uplifting environment, as well as with an intrusive and intentional network of student-support services. However, as discussed in chapter 3, the data at HBCUs continues to lag behind data at majority institutions when it comes to retention and graduation rates.

How is it that the graduation rates for blacks and minority students at majority institutions (TWIs) are frequently better than the graduation rates for blacks and minorities at HBCUs? Besides the most obvious contributing factors of household income and socioeconomic status, academic preparedness and remediation levels, and the selectivity of institutions, it can be argued that HBCUs simply lack the strategic, "on-purpose" programs and initiatives designed to raise and improve retention and graduation rates.

## COMMON ACADEMIC-SUPPORT PROGRAMS

At Morgan State University, just like at so many other HBCUs and colleges and universities in general, myriad programs are offered to support students. Offices all across campus offer programs to help acclimate students to the college campus culture. These initiatives include summer programs, tutoring programs, and mentoring programs.

One of the most popular types of programs offered is the black-male initiative. Palmer, Davis, and Hilton (2009) conclude that issues such as lack of financial assistance, the inability of black males to use campus support services, and problems in homes and communities are factors that posed challenges to their academic success in spite of the existence of black-male initiatives and programs offered on the campuses of most HBCUs.

While these programs are often assessed using self-reported data from student participants to include surveys and focus groups, it is difficult to correlate many of these programs with increased graduation rates. Even when associations can be made between participation in a summer bridge, tutoring, or mentoring programs and retention and graduation rates, the participant base often is limited to a small number of students. These programs have intrinsic value; students, faculty, and staff who participate in these programs typically report that they feel rewarded and more engaged with the institution.

Morgan State University, like so many colleges, has a long-standing history of providing for student programs aimed at increasing student success. These programs include workshops for students who are on academic probation, roundtable discussions with faculty and staff, town hall meetings to air out concerns with senior administrators and staff, honors programs and societies, male-only initiatives, female-only initiatives, programs for commuter students, first-generation college-going initiatives, peer-to-peer programs, veterans services and support, nontraditional student programs, support for single parents and families, career-readiness initiatives, and many other programs designed for specific subpopulations of students.

Karagiannis, Herring, and Williams's (2014) findings suggest that students who seek help in academic-support programs such as tutoring and/or learning centers do earn higher grades than those students who do not participate in such programs; however, they fail to make a correlation between the grades earned in specific courses and subsequent retention, graduation, and completion rates. The question for administrators with oversight and leadership over these academic-support programs is which of these programs can be tied directly to increased retention and graduation rates for the student participants engaged in each program or initiative?

## ARE THEY WORKING?

It is highly recommended that every higher education professional ask this question at their respective institution. What was discovered at Morgan State University was that even though these programs were evaluated and measured based on staff and administrators' feelings of fulfillment and satisfaction as administrators, as well as based on the self-reported data obtained from student participants, it was very difficult to track long-term student outcomes and metrics and subsequently tie them back to participation in these

programs. Moreover, for many years, Morgan experienced declining retention and graduation rates while these programs and initiatives thrived.

The Office of Student Success and Retention (OSSR) staff at Morgan
State University were challenged to take inventory of every program in
their respective college or school and eliminate programs that could not be
directly associated with increased student success as measured by retention
and graduation rates.

What was discovered was twofold: (1) many of the student participants in
these "feel-good" programs were not in a retention/graduation cohort as measured by IPEDS either because they were transfer, nontraditional, or part-time
students, or because they had begun college in terms or semesters other than
the fall semester, or because the students already had been counted against the
institution because the six-year window for their matriculation had passed;
or (2) student participants in the programs did not have significantly higher
retention and/or graduation rates than their nonparticipating student peers.

## THE GENESIS OF STRATEGIC PROGRAMMING AT MSU

In 2010, the director of institutional research (IR) at Morgan shared some data
with senior staff from the National Student Clearinghouse (www.student-
clearinghouse.org). More than 3,600 postsecondary institutions enrolling 98
percent of all students at all two-year and four-year, both public and private,
institutions are members of the National Student Clearinghouse. Through the
clearinghouse, institutions can track student enrollment among institutions
including transfer students and "stop-outs."

Obtaining data from the clearinghouse would foster an investigation into
the status of many "missing" or stopped-out students at Morgan, especially
students who were counted in the retention and graduation cohorts. Stop-
outs are students who do not necessarily withdraw officially from a college
or university but rather simply are not enrolled for one or more semesters.
Stopping-out at HBCUs is not uncommon.

What was shocking was the number of Morgan students who were not
enrolled at Morgan but who had not transferred to any other institution; these
Morgan students had left Morgan in good academic standing with a minimum
cumulative GPA of 2.0, and many had earned junior- or senior-level clas-
sification status.

The initial intent in requesting the data from the IR director was to "find"
Morgan students in an effort to better understand the types of institutions students may be transferring to; for example, some out-of-state students return
home to attend a less expensive four-year college, or some students choose to

matriculate at a two-year institution for a period of time to earn general education credits at a reduced cost. Again, what was amazing was that students in the graduation cohorts were stopped-out, in good academic standing, with credits amassed, but were not matriculating at any other institution among the 3,600+ National Student Clearinghouse member institutions.

This is consistent with DesJardins, Ahlburg, and McCall's finding that "those who fail to graduate do so as the consequence of a rational economic choice. . . . The graduation decision is part of the overall labor market optimizing problem. . . . It is incorrect to view those who fail to graduate as primarily a failure on the part of the university. . . . Failure to graduate does not necessarily reflect a lack of ability on the part of the student" (2002, p. 556).

## A BRIGHT IDEA IS BORN

I shared the National Student Clearinghouse data with our associate provost, and she recommended that I present this data to our new, incoming college president with my idea to "reclaim" stopped-out students in a direct attempt to improve our cohort graduation rate.

True story: I had left my cellular phone carrier to go to a different provider. Shortly thereafter, I received a letter in the mail from my old cell phone provider that read, "We want you back," and it included a list of benefits that I would be eligible for if I were to return to them and sign a new contract. I could get a free new phone, more data, more storage, more minutes, and so on.

I immediately thought about applying the "we want you back" campaign strategy to stopped-out Morgan students. The new initiative at Morgan State University would be known as the Reclamation Initiative.

## THE RECLAMATION INITIATIVE

The MSU Reclamation Initiative was created specifically to address the need to increase six-year graduation rates. By identifying students who were in good academic standing but were no longer enrolled, Morgan State University increased the 2005 cohort graduation rate of 28.9 percent to 30.2 percent for the 2006 cohort. During the 2011–2012 academic year, forty students from the fall 2006 first-time, full-time cohort not currently enrolled at Morgan were sent letters inviting them to return to the university to complete their degree requirements in time for graduation in May of 2012.

After sending the letters, because of the short turnaround in terms of time before the start of spring 2012 classes, calls were placed to each student to inquire about his or her interest in returning to Morgan. Students reported leaving Morgan due to reductions in funding (grants, loans, scholarships), emergency or personal circumstances, and promotions or offers of full-time employment on their jobs. Of the forty students to be reclaimed during the first year of the program, thirty were in-state students and ten were out-of-state students; sixteen were female and twenty-four were male students.

## THE RESULTS ARE IN. . . .

The Reclamation Initiative, now in its fifth year of implementation at Morgan State University, has reached out to forty students from the incoming fall 2006 freshman cohort, thirty-one students from the incoming fall 2007 freshman cohort, forty-two students from the incoming fall 2008 freshman cohort, and twenty students from the fall 2009 cohort resulting in the re-enrollment of fifty-six students.

Eleven of the nineteen Reclamation students from the fall 2006 cohort graduated on time by May of 2012, nine of the seventeen Reclamation students from the fall 2007 cohort graduated on time by May of 2013, and nine of the eighteen Reclamation students from the fall 2008 cohort graduated on time by May of 2014.

Having funding ($50,000) designated especially for students who have stopped-out at some point, earned 90+ credits with at least a 2.0 cumulative GPA, and been officially audited by their dean or department for graduation has been a targeted, strategic approach to increasing college completion rates at Morgan. Many of the 2006–2008 cohort students in their fifth and sixth year of college had already invested anywhere from $42,000 to $144,000 in loans to pay for their college education.

Although 96 percent of Morgan's undergraduate student population receives some type of financial aid (grant, loan, scholarship, etc.), very few students get 100 percent of their tuition and fees paid by financial aid. Thus, many students work part-time or full-time to supplement their cost of attendance. Working, in many instances, leads to decreased progress toward degree completion especially for students who report working more hours over time, or students who get promoted on their jobs.

## A MODEL PROGRAM

With plans to continue and expand the Reclamation Initiative, Morgan applied for and was awarded an MHEC (Maryland Higher Education Commission) One Step Away grant for near-completers in 2012. The MHEC One Step Away grant was a byproduct of Morgan's Reclamation Initiative in the state of Maryland.

After reporting the aforementioned results of Morgan's ongoing program to "reclaim" stopped-out students to the legislature in the 2011 and 2012 annual reports, MHEC patterned the One Step Away grant after the best practices and lessons learned from the program in the context of a growing national understanding of the near-completer population and its undeniable connection to retention, graduation, and completion rates.

"Crossing the Finish Line: A National Effort to Address Near Completion," a report published by the Institute for Higher Education Policy in 2011, concluded that this population of students (stopped-out near-completers):

> represent[s] the low-hanging fruit in our national agenda to increase the number of college graduates. Policies and practices designed to reach and support these students through completion have the potential to move the needle on our collective efforts to increase college completion for all students. . . . To move the needle on near completion, college and universities will be on the front line to identify near completers, award degrees for "eligibles," and develop degree completion plans that successfully reengage and graduate students. (p. 5)

Since 2012, the Maryland One Step Away grant for "near-completers" has only further enhanced and supported the existing Reclamation Initiative at Morgan by providing additional resources to degree-eligible and degree-potential students. The grant has expanded academic, financial, and social advising supports that facilitate successful re-enrollment and subsequent degree completion.

## ONE STEP AWAY

The state of Maryland defines *degree-eligible students* as students who have stopped-out but may not realize that they already have met the minimum requirements for a degree and are eligible for graduation perhaps with only the need to complete a simple administrative process. The state of Maryland defines *degree-potential students* as students who are close to completing their degree with less than one academic year left to finish before graduation. All Morgan student participants in the Reclamation Initiative are degree-potential students.

With foreseeable plans to continue the institutional commitment to provide much-needed financial support ($50,000 per academic year) with concierge re-enrollment services to near-completers, Morgan proposed in a second MHEC One Step Away grant application to invest in much-needed degree-auditing software to promote degree completion for near-completers.

After winning a second MHEC One Step Away grant, Morgan took one "giant" step toward long-term success by using the grant for near-completers to invest in comprehensive degree-auditing software to assist near completers in obtaining their official degree audit and an "exit strategy" for degree completion.

## AN EXIT STRATEGY

After four years of experience with reclaiming near-completers, the one consistent challenge Morgan has had was obtaining an official degree audit and an "exit strategy" for students attempting to re-enroll. As is the case with too many postsecondary institutions in the United States, Morgan State University still used 100 percent manual degree-auditing in each academic department, school, and college. Individuals (evaluators) used a variety of hard-copy forms developed in their departments to evaluate students' progress in their degree program.

Typically, students are given this hard-copy degree plan as freshmen, and they carry it around with them for the next four, five, or six years. Multiple copies of this form are made every time a student meets with his or her academic advisor. Finally, when students apply for graduation, an "official" senior credit audit is requested by the Office of Records and Registration from the dean and/or chairperson of the student's department.

The designated official (evaluator) in the school or department uses another hard-copy form to evaluate students' transcripts in Banner (Morgan's student information system) to determine their eligibility for graduation, as well as their status in their academic program. This is a long, detailed, and tedious process for the evaluator, as well as for the students and advisors waiting to obtain the official degree audit.

In working with stopped-out students attempting to re-enroll at the university, the most challenging issue had been the obtaining of official degree audits from the department, school, or college. The Reclamation Initiative program director had to write memos and "official" emails to request degree audits for every near-completer to include a justification for each request. Except for the initial hard copy of a student's four-year degree plan that they received from their academic advisor in their first year, students have had no way of knowing their status in their degree program on a semester-by-semester basis.

This lack of information is especially difficult for stop-out students and near-completers. Many times their degree program has changed or has been modified in terms of course requirements. Waiting for an official degree audit delays students' time to graduation and creates a sense of unnecessary frustration. Best practices suggest that students should always know and/or have access to their status in their degree program.

## DEGREE-AUDITING SOFTWARE

As mentioned before, Morgan decided to take one "giant" step toward long-term success by using the new (second) Maryland One Step Away grant for near-completers to invest in much-needed degree-auditing software to assist near-completers in obtaining their official degree audit and an "exit strategy" for degree completion.

Arroyo and Gasman (2014) rightly have stated that for institutions, "rather than blaming so-called underperforming black students, understanding the essential institutional components and processes for facilitating their success is imperative" (p. 60). Degree-auditing technology is one such imperative component for facilitating student success.

For Morgan, as well as for any college or university, the benefits of investing in degree-auditing software are:

1. enabling the institution to accelerate degree-audit approvals;
2. improving the overall quality of the students'/near-completers' experience through user-friendly on-demand features like degree shopping; and
3. providing a robust, scalable, and configurable campus-wide solution that meets all requirements of the degree-auditing process.

Additional long-term benefits of degree-auditing software include: students not wasting time and money on unnecessary courses; reducing students' stress level about graduating on time; providing advisors and evaluators with more time to share insightful advice that supports better student outcomes; monitoring course demand and offering the right classes at the right time for near-completers; and integrating the software with the student information system (Banner) so that interactions with students are recorded for the students, their faculty, and their advisors to access degree-monitoring and degree-shopping features.

Degree shopping enables students to compare their progress in one degree program or major field of study to other degree programs or major fields of study at an institution so that students can make informed decisions as to how to progress and persist toward degree completion. After presenting documented success with Morgan's Reclamation Initiative, funding a comprehensive degree-auditing system that will promote degree completion by providing easy access to interactive (live) degree plans for students, faculty, and advisors was the next logical step.

## OTHER STRATEGIC INITIATIVES

Following the successful implementation of the Reclamation Initiative and the One Step Away grant(s), Morgan began a wider campaign to "welcome home" all stopped-out students from every cohort, not just near-completers. "Welcome Home Day" is now an annual event designed to invite any and all stopped-out students back to re-enroll in a "one-stop shop" environment where they can meet with an advisor, register for classes, and handle their obligations (re-admittance, financial aid, housing, etc.) all in one place, on one day.

## THE GENESIS OF A PHILOSOPHY

Our associate provost acted as a catalyst for this new philosophy of "reclaiming everybody"; she had observed how grateful students were after receiving an invitation to come back to Morgan. My office shelves are filled with handwritten "thank you" notes from our re-enrolled students! I had provided her case-by-case details about how much less the funding support actually meant to students in comparison to the concierge-level one-on-one engagement with me and my staff, as well as compared to the guidance provided to returning students in terms of how to navigate specific processes throughout the university.

In other words, the "hand-holding" and "exit-strategy" approach went a long way with students, even more so than the funding set aside to support these students. In fact, many students discovered that their financial situation actually had improved during their stop-out; for example, some students now were employed full-time, or now they were a parent, or perhaps they were married—all factors that improved their eligibility for certain types of financial aid, grants, loans, and scholarships.

## MOVING THE DATA

As the postsecondary community awaits an updated and improved IPEDS reporting system, higher education professionals and practitioners are strongly encouraged to design programs similar to Morgan's Reclamation Initiative that aim strategically at "moving the data." This approach requires that staff and administrators first know who is in "the cohort" of first-time, full-time freshmen for every fall term or semester, as discussed in chapter 3; that the cohorts be systematically tracked and monitored, as discussed chapter 5; and that programs are created to foster student success for these students, success that can be measured and directly correlated to increased retention, graduation, and completion rates.

According to Lee and Keys (2013), "The HBCUs that will survive in the ever-changing landscape of higher education will be those that develop visionary strategies for their institutions" (p. 24). Besides the Reclamation Initiative, Morgan State University has a summer catch-up program that pays for students in the School of Engineering to take one or two courses during the Summer I or Summer II terms, courses that they failed during the fall or spring semesters, so that they can "catch up" and not fall behind in their curriculum sequence as a result of repeating courses. Too many students fall behind because of one or more prerequisite courses, and they are never able to "catch up" with the progress of peers in their cohort.

One more of these "on-purpose" strategic initiatives at Morgan State University is the Institutional Aid program. Many colleges and universities award need-based institutional aid to students to close the gap between their financial-aid package and their EFC (estimated family contribution) for their cost of attendance. Morgan State University uses the cohort designation of students as one of the criteria for an institutional aid award so that students in the retention and graduation cohorts receive priority funding, and these students are required to complete service hours on campus that foster engagement with faculty, staff, and administrators.

## BECOMING AND REMAINING STRATEGIC

HBCUs and other institutions of higher education can afford to become more intentional and strategic, especially considering the limited resources available at many HBCUs. Postsecondary institutions are admonished to take an inventory of all programs and initiatives and ask the question that was asked at Morgan State University, "Which of these programs can be tied directly to increased retention and graduation rates for the student participants engaged in each program or initiative?"

From there, let the data, best practices, and strategic innovation inform the "on-purpose" development of effective student success programs. In the Education Trust report, *Learning From High-Performing and Fast-Gaining*

*Institutions: Top 10 Analyses to Provoke Discussion and Action on College Completion*, Yeado, Haycock, Johnstone, and Chaplot end their study with this conclusion:

> Indeed, if anything is clear from the experiences of campuses that are on sustained improvement trajectories, it is that they have made the transition from seeing the demographics of their students as destiny to understanding that colleges really can, through sustained efforts, radically reshape their student success rates without becoming more selective. (p. 15)

## CHAPTER 6: QUESTIONS AND NEXT STEPS

1. Take an inventory of all academic-support and student success programs and initiatives at the institution.
2. When and how are these programs and initiatives evaluated and measured?
3. Can any of these programs be directly correlated to increased retention and graduation rates for the student participants engaged in each program or initiative?
4. Obtain the data for the postsecondary institution from the National Student Clearinghouse to track stopped-out and no-longer-enrolled students.
5. Design a customized program for stopped-out students and/or near-completers to facilitate re-enrollment and engagement with the institution.
6. Outline an "exit strategy" for students to include official degree audits and intrusive academic advisement.
7. Develop a long-term plan to become more intentional and strategic, resulting in effective student success programs that increase retention and graduation rates as measured by the IPEDS standard.

## REFERENCES

Arroyo, A. T., & Gasman, M. (November 2014). An HBCU-Based Educational Approach for Black College Student Success: Toward a Framework with Implications for All Institutions. *American Journal of Education, 121*(1), 57–85.

DesJardins, S. L., Ahlburg, D. A., & McCall, B. P. (September/October 2002). A Temporal Investigation of Factors Related to Timely Degree Completion. *Journal of Higher Education, 73*(5), 555–81.

Institute for Higher Education Policy (October 2011). Crossing the Finish Line: A National Effort to Address Near Completion. Washington, DC: Institute for Higher Education Policy.

Karagiannis, N., Herring, II, R. A., & Williams, M. T. (April 2014). Challenges Facing Student Learning at HBCUs Today: An Exploratory Investigation. *International Journal of Humanities and Social Science, 4*(6), 181–91.

Lee Jr., J. M., & Keys, S. W. (2013). *Repositioning HBCUs for the Future: Access, Success, Research & Innovation.* Washington, DC: Association of Public and Land-Grant Universities (APLU), Office of Access and Success Discussion Paper 2013-01.

Offenstein, J., & Shulock, N. (2009). *Community College Student Outcomes: Limitations of the Integrated Postsecondary Education Data System (IPEDS) and Recommendations for Improvement.* Sacramento: Institute for Higher Education Leadership & Policy at California State University, Sacramento.

Palmer, R. T., Davis, R. J., & Hilton, A. A. (July/August 2009). Exploring Challenges That Threaten to Impede the Academic Success of Academically Underprepared Black Males at an HBCU. *Journal of College Student Development*, *50*(4), 429–45.

Yeado, J., Haycock, K., Johnstone, R., & Chaplot, P. (January 2014). *Learning from High-Performing and Fast-Gaining Institutions: Top 10 Analyses to Provoke Discussion and Action on College Completion.* The Education Trust. Available at http://collegecampaign.org/wp-content/uploads/2014/06/PracticeGuide.pdf.

# Chapter Seven

# Leveraging External Resources

## *Getting the Most Out of Grants*

Morgan State University, just like so many other HBCUs, long has been the beneficiary of external grants and funding. HBCUs have been largely successful in securing federal grants from the U.S. Department of Education, the U.S. Department of Housing and Urban Development (HUD), the National Institutes of Health (NIH), the National Science Foundation (NSF), the Centers for Disease Control and Prevention (CDC), the National Endowment for the Humanities (NEH), the Substance Abuse and Mental Health Services Administration (SAMHSA), the National Park Service, and other federal agencies. The White House Initiative on Historically Black Colleges and Universities' website lists federal funding opportunities for HBCUs: www. ed.gov/edblogs/whhbcu/federal-grant-opportunities.

Specifically in the fields of science, technology, engineering, and mathematics (STEM), HBCUs have competed for and won prestigious research grants. In 2014, Morgan State University won a $23.3 million award, the second largest competitive award in its history and the highest from the National Institutes of Health (Adebola, 2014). In any fiscal year, Morgan receives approximately $30 million dollars of external funding from grants and sponsored programs with the greatest proportion of funding in the STEM disciplines.

Funding in the STEM fields continues to expand to include new and innovative fields such as alternative energy, climate change, green architecture, and cybersecurity. In 2014, Vice President Joe Biden announced a cybersecurity grant and partnership with minority-serving institutions that created another funding opportunity for HBCUs (The White House, 2015). The Department of Energy will provide a $25 million grant over the next five years to support cybersecurity education at thirteen HBCUs, two national labs, and a K–12 school district (Rhodes, 2015).

While grant and funding opportunities at federal and state agencies are available to HBCUs, a number of HBCUs have forged partnerships in the private sector as well. Private partners such as the Home Depot, Lockheed Martin Corporation, and Regions Financial offer grant opportunities to HBCUs aimed at helping to preserve and improve some of America's most historic campuses and landmarks, assisting HBCUs through subcontracting opportunities, technology transfer, cooperative education programs, and other collaborative initiatives, and supporting financial education, academics, athletics, and alumni engagement (Franklin, 2014; Lockheed Martin, 2013; "Boeing, Lockheed," 2003; "Regions Financial," 2012).

In the 2010 policy brief *Comprehensive Funding Approaches for Historically Black Colleges and Universities*, Dr. Marybeth Gasman concludes:

> Funders at the state and federal level as well as private funders should direct their support toward investments in infrastructure, including the fundraising infrastructure of HBCUs. A better infrastructure attracts more alumni support, helps to build endowment, and in effect, builds momentum among institutional constituents. (p. 6)

When it comes to retention, graduation, and college completion at HBCUs, some of the best partners are found in the not-for-profit sector. Partners such as the Lumina Foundation, the Bill & Melinda Gates Foundation, the Thurgood Marshall College Fund (TMCF), the Southern Education Foundation (SEF), USA Funds, the Institute for Higher Education Policy (IHEP), the Kresge Foundation, and the United Negro College Fund (UNCF) provide funding opportunities specifically designed to help improve retention and graduation rates, academic programming, and student academic support. Grants from these not-for-profit organizations can be used to supplement the costs of tutoring, academic coaching, summer programs, supplemental instruction, and technology.

According to *Top Strategic Issues Facing HBCUs, Now and into the Future*, a 2014 report by the Association of Governing Boards of Universities and Colleges:

> Presidents are grappling with how to find cost-effective ways to ensure student success. Limited resources affect many institutions' abilities to offer adequate support services for the large number of students in need of additional guidance or remediation. . . . Providing adequate support programs does not just benefit those who are underprepared. (p. 7)

The Morgan State University Office of Student Success and Retention (OSSR) has been the beneficiary of strategic partnerships and grants from the Bill & Melinda Gates Foundation, the Maryland Higher Education

Commission (MHEC), and AmeriCorps*Vista that have helped to promote increases in retention as well as improvements in the delivery of academic support services.

These grants have played an instrumental role in Morgan's maintaining a retention rate above 70 percent for four consecutive years by providing momentum, generating excitement, leveraging financial resources, and driving culture change in the delivery of student academic support at the university.

## GRANTS ARE WORTH MUCH MORE THAN MONEY

I am a firm believer in the power and leverage that external grants and funding bring to a college campus, especially an HBCU. Notably, grants bring financial resources to the table, resources often unavailable within an institution's operating budget. However, the intangible benefits of external grants and funding are immeasurable.

Presidents and campus leaders already have generated long lists of institutional priorities for faculty, students, and administrators that require commitments of financial resources, but more so of human resources. It takes more than just money for any new program, initiative, or campus-wide implementation to launch; it takes time and energy.

Even though staff and administrators often send great ideas and new innovations forward to senior campus leaders, without funding and the commitment of personnel to support these ideas, they will not find their way to the top of long priority lists. In the areas of retention, student success, and college completion, we often run short on funding and time and energy to facilitate new programs and initiatives.

Here's where external funding and grants can "save the day" and act as a catalyst to push the institution forward. Securing a competitive grant from an outside resource brings not only money to the institution, but also leverage, branding, recognition, commitment, and leadership. There's no better way to promote a student success agenda at your institution than to bring the name recognition, the external leverage, and the money of an outside agency, foundation, or company to the table.

Once the institution is awarded a reputable and prestigious competitive grant, the supportive campus infrastructure, stakeholders, key personnel, and senior leadership are likely to "get behind" and fully support the new study, program, initiative, and/or technology. Many of the new retention and success initiatives at Morgan State University would not have happened without senior staff and administrators securing external grants and funding to not only support the initiatives financially, but also elevate the initiatives to the top of the campus-wide agenda.

The winning grant proposals that I have written to the Maryland Higher Education Commission, the Bill & Melinda Gates Foundation, and Maryland-DC Campus Compact AmeriCorps*VISTA detailed in this chapter sparked momentum to move forward ideas and programs that would otherwise not have been campus-wide priorities. We authored other grant proposals that were not successful such as the MSI Models of Success grant proposal, but we never gave up.

You should recognize grant writing as an ongoing tool to promote student success on your campus with the understanding that if you keep writing, eventually you will win. Often the perceived benefits of competitive grants are associated with faculty and research at institutions, but I highly recommend that student academic-support staff and administrators activate and maximize this strategy.

## PUBLIC GRANTS:
## FUNDING THAT'S A STRONG FOUNDATION

The OSSR applied for and was awarded the MHEC's One Step Away grant for "near-completers" in 2012. The total grant award was a modest $43,180 for a period of January 2013 until January 2015. The Maryland One Step Away grant for "near-completers" enhanced and supported the existing Reclamation Initiative at MSU by providing additional resources to degree-eligible and degree-potential students and by expanding academic, financial, and social advising supports that facilitate successful re-enrollment and subsequent degree completion.

A Maryland StateStat press release, "Nearly 300 Students Back in the Classroom in First Phase of the One Step Away Program," reported that some students needed less than $1,000 to pay off a parking ticket or library fine to get back in the classroom.

This innovative project created an opportunity for students who had left the university in good academic standing with a 2.0 GPA or better and had earned at least ninety credits to return in their fifth or sixth academic year to finish Morgan "on time" in six consecutive years or less. Morgan used the MHEC One Step Away grant to: (1) provide financial support to these students directly; and (2) enrich the peer-to-peer tutoring experience for these returning students. The Reclamation Initiative at MSU has a proven track record of success in promoting degree completion.

With plans to continue and expand the Reclamation Initiative, Morgan's OSSR applied for and was awarded a second MHEC One Step Away grant for near-completers in the amount of $75,000. Although having funding designated especially for near-completers who have stopped-out at some point is a targeted, strategic approach to increasing college-completion rates at Morgan, a longer-term solution for near-completers was the next logical step for the Reclamation Initiative.

With a commitment to continue Morgan's institutional goal to provide much-needed financial support with concierge re-enrollment services to near-completers, the OSSR proposed to invest in much-needed degree-auditing software to promote degree completion for near-completers.

Morgan is taking one "giant" step toward long-term success by using the second MHEC One Step Away grant for near-completers to invest in degree-auditing software to assist near-completers in obtaining their official degree audit and an "exit strategy" for degree completion. Morgan's OSSR utilizes this public funding opportunity to further develop and improve its existing outreach strategies to inform and encourage near-completers to re-enroll in college as well as to enhance the student-support systems to include academic, financial, and/or social advising and supports that facilitate smooth reentry into the educational environment and retention through to degree completion.

## AMERICORPS*VISTA: A NONTRADITIONAL GRANT FOR AN HBCU

In 2011, the OSSR won a three-year AmeriCorps*VISTA grant through Maryland-DC Campus Compact (MDCCC) to employ a full-time AmeriCorps*VISTA volunteer in the position of financial-literacy coordinator (valued at $45,000 per year) in the OSSR for three years. Volunteers in Service to America (VISTA) was founded in 1965 as a national service program to fight poverty in America. In 1993, VISTA was incorporated into the AmeriCorps network of programs. Today, more than seven thousand Americans volunteer annually to support community efforts to overcome poverty (Bryer, Augustin, Barve, Gracia, and Perez, 2013).

The vision for the OSSR Financial Literacy Program is to reverse the cycle of low family income and socioeconomic status by enhancing the financial literacy of students and their families, thereby increasing students' retention and graduation rates. To fulfill this vision, Morgan fostered partnerships with PNC Bank, the FDIC, USA Funds, MDCCC, and AmeriCorps*VISTA—all at no additional cost to the university.

The AmeriCorps*VISTA's role included (1) researching, developing, and facilitating the financial literacy aspects of the program based on existing, successful financial literacy model programs, (2) coordinating the service project for the students in partnership with PNC Bank, (3) recruiting and coordinating the peer mentors for the program, and (4) investigating possible sources of funding for scholarships for program completers.

PNC Bank serves as Morgan's designated community partner for the MDCCC AmeriCorps*VISTA grant and sponsors the workshops Foundations of Money Management, Budgeting, and Credit every semester. As Morgan's on-campus bank, PNC collaborates with the OSSR in every aspect of the program including sponsoring Dr. DeForest Soaries, author of *dfree: Breaking Free from Financial Slavery*, to kick off the Financial Literacy Program each fall; he speaks to and inspires an audience of more than four hundred students every October.

Students have provided positive feedback following the kick-off symposium including their desire to save money by "paying themselves first," reduce their credit card usage, pay their bills on time, pay more than their minimum payments, and pay cash for the things that they want.

As a supplement to the AmeriCorps*VISTA grant, Morgan State University was selected by the White House Initiative on HBCUs to partner with the FDIC and the MoneySmart curriculum to deliver financial education to Morgan students. Sixteen peer ambassadors (volunteers) are trained by the FDIC each academic year to provide the MoneySmart curriculum to students in conjunction with the PNC Bank workshops coordinated by the AmeriCorps*VISTA.

Three of Morgan's athletic teams (football, volleyball, and track) have been mandated to participate in the Financial Literacy Program. In January 2013, Morgan State University's financial-literacy program was featured in an article—"Morgan State Promotes Financial Literacy"—in *Diverse: Issues in Higher Education* (Gasman).

## A GAME-CHANGER: THE BILL & MELINDA GATES FOUNDATION IPAS GRANT

In spring of 2013, Morgan State University submitted a grant proposal and was awarded a $100,000 grant from the Bill & Melinda Gates Foundation for the implementation of Integrated Planning and Advising Services (IPAS) technology. As one of only nineteen selected institutions and the only HBCU, Morgan partnered with Starfish Retention Solutions to automate its Early Alert and Response System for faculty, staff, and students. IPAS technology has enhanced advising and provides sophisticated, yet user-friendly, tracking and monitoring systems for the university. Morgan also served as one of the seven funded institutions to participate in an intense, longitudinal research cohort to be evaluated by the Bill & Melinda Gates Foundation for effective implementation and integration of campus-wide IPAS technology (Karp & Fletcher, 2014).

In preparing a proposal in response to the Bill & Melinda Gates Foundation request for proposal, Morgan assembled a team of campus stakeholders to determine its readiness for IPAS implementation. These campus stakeholders included the Office of Residence Life and Housing, the University Honors Program, the Transfer Center, the IT Department, the Office of Institutional Advancement, the Office of Institutional Research, the Center for Academic Success and Achievement, and the OSSR. All stakeholders and campus collaborators agreed unanimously that it was Morgan's time and season for IPAS technology.

Departments and their representatives committed resources and time to complete the adoption of IPAS technology by spring 2014. The first goal in Morgan State University's strategic plan is to enhance student success. Being awarded an IPAS grant for technology from the Bill & Melinda Gates Foundation has acted as a catalyst toward achieving this goal. This was an ideal opportunity for Morgan State University, especially for the OSSR, to make progress toward its goal of increasing retention and graduation rates.

The following not-for-profit organizations have proven track records in partnering with HBCUs to promote student success and degree completion:

## LUMINA FOUNDATION

Lumina Foundation (www.luminafoundation.org) is the nation's largest private foundation focused solely on increasing Americans' success in higher education, awarding more than sixteen hundred grants since its inception in 2000. The Lumina Foundation is committed to increasing the proportion of Americans with high-quality degrees, certificates, and other credentials to 60 percent by 2025 (known as Goal 2025). The Lumina Foundation's outcomes-based approach focuses on helping to design and build an accessible, responsive, and accountable higher education system while fostering a national sense of urgency for action to achieve "Goal 2025."

Even though a large majority of Lumina grants are awarded to partners solicited by the foundation based on unique capacity or position to leverage large-scale systemic change, a modest amount of grant funding is allocated each year for unsolicited inquiries to encourage innovative ideas that relate to the strategic portfolio.

The Lumina Foundation has provided funding to support the Minority-Serving Institutions Models of Success Program, Building Engagement and Attainment for Minority Students, and the Historically Black Colleges and Universities Innovation and Entrepreneurship Collaborative (the HBCU Collaborative).

## BILL & MELINDA GATES FOUNDATION

The Bill & Melinda Gates Foundation (www.gatesfoundation.org/What-We-Do/US-Program/Postsecondary-Success) is committed to ensuring postsecondary success by working to dramatically increase the number of young people who obtain a postsecondary degree or certificate with labor-market value. The Bill & Melinda Gates Foundation postsecondary success strategy seeks to increase low-income students' college completion rates through innovations that can improve the productivity and performance of U.S. universities and colleges and ensure that all students have access to a high-quality, highly personalized education.

The Gates Foundation offers grants and funding opportunities that aim at dramatically increasing community-college completion rates, that work to find postsecondary financial-aid solutions, and that support a range of innovators from within and outside the postsecondary education system who are creating options and technology that support the busy lives of today's college students, enabling them to earn a credential with value in the labor market without incurring significant debt.

## UNITED NEGRO COLLEGE FUND

Since its founding in 1944, the United Negro College Fund (UNCF, www.uncf.org) has raised more than $3.6 billion to help more than 400,000 students receive college degrees at UNCF member institutions. UNCF provides financial support for its thirty-seven member HBCUs for scholarships and capacity building. The Institute for Capacity Building, launched in 2006 by UNCF, helps HBCUs draw on their foundations of existing institutional strength and potential by offering institutional funding such as planning and implementation grants.

The Annenberg Foundation awarded the UNCF a $2 million grant that has benefited a total of ten member colleges and universities through a competitive selection process. The grants assist selected, eligible member colleges and universities to improve and strengthen the recruitment and retention of minority students interested in becoming teachers, to create K–12 collaborative partnerships aimed to improve education programs for those students majoring in education, to provide training and professional development to enhance teaching techniques and improve learning outcomes of K–12 students and college students interested in becoming teachers, and to increase the use of technology in teaching venues.

## THURGOOD MARSHALL COLLEGE FUND

Established in 1987, the Thurgood Marshall College Fund (TMCF, www. thurgoodmarshallfund.net) is named for the U.S. Supreme Court's first African-American justice. The TMCF, having raised over $200 million to date for programmatic, capacity-building support and scholarships, supports and represents nearly 300,000 students attending its forty-seven member-schools that include public HBCUs, medical schools, and law schools. The TMCF has offered grants to develop science or engineering projects including the TMCF Technology Initiative, which was created to address long-term technology needs of HBCU campuses and to identify funding sources to support technology upgrades.

## THE KRESGE FOUNDATION

The Kresge Foundation (http://kresge.org) is a $3 billion private, national foundation headquartered in Metropolitan Detroit that works to expand opportunities in America's cities through grant making and investing in arts and culture, education, environment, health, and human services. The Kresge HBCU Initiative was a five-year, $18 million program created and funded to help five HBCUs develop comprehensive advancement programs.

The initiative provided each institution with specialized funding, along with training and technical assistance, to help them develop stronger self-sustaining advancement operations. At the end of the initiative, the five grantees (HBCUs) had greatly increased the amount of money raised from private sources such as alumni, trustees, and individuals, and each grantee had a comprehensive advancement program with adequate staffing, greatly improved technology, standard policies and procedures, and an ongoing and continuous program of prospect cultivation (Schulze, 2005).

## SOUTHERN EDUCATION FOUNDATION

The Southern Education Foundation (SEF, www.southerneducation.org) uses collaboration, advocacy, and research to improve outcomes from early childhood to adulthood and advance equity and excellence in education for all students in the South, particularly low-income students and students of color. SEF's higher education efforts are designed to address a range of issues that influence student success and degree attainment among low-income and minority students.

The MSI Consortium for Innovation and Change is designed to highlight and support state-of-the-art initiatives that promise to improve institutional practice and outcomes for students. SEF identifies and engages institutions that have deep interest and/or investment in enhancing practices that directly improve student success.

SEF's Improving College Access and Completion strategy examines and reports on policies that impact participation, retention, and degree completion; establishes demonstration projects that serve as laboratories for testing innovative practices that hold the promise of increasing degree completion; convenes institutional leaders and university trustees to share evidence-based practices that include institutional effectiveness; and provides technical assistance and capacity building to institutions to enhance program effectiveness and student learning outcomes.

## USA FUNDS

USA Funds (www.usafunds.org) has adopted "Completion with a Purpose" as the guiding principle for its philanthropic and investment activities, supporting initiatives that are focused on transforming the higher education experience for America's students so they are prepared for jobs in the twenty-first-century economy. "Completion with a Purpose" means building a more purposeful path for students to, and through, college and onto rewarding careers and successful lives.

USA Funds is focused on initiatives in these key areas:

1. streamlining key education transitions;
2. facilitating smoother pathways from campus to the workplace;
3. promoting innovative approaches to college and career preparation;
4. building new frameworks for data-driven decision making.

USA Funds provides philanthropic support to and engages in partnerships with selected state governments and metropolitan areas, national organizations, as well as colleges and universities and community-based organizations that share its vision of "Completion with a Purpose."

## INSTITUTE FOR HIGHER EDUCATION POLICY

In 2013, the Institute for Higher Education Policy (IHEP, www.ihep.org) celebrated its twentieth anniversary by announcing the IHEP Champions of Access and Success Awards to honor the postsecondary institutions and individuals who have successfully advanced strategies that increase opportunity, persistence, and degree completion for underserved students.

IHEP serves as a resource for government agencies, higher education organizations, philanthropic foundations, and others committed to increasing access and success in postsecondary education by offering policy recommendations and unique research in order to foster solutions to the access and success challenges facing today's students. Financial support for IHEP is provided by philanthropic organizations, along with some funding from state governments, foreign governments, and others who are working to advance access in higher education.

In 2008, IHEP partnered with Walmart to offer Minority Student Success Awards ($100,000 grant per institution) to help build success in enrolling, retaining, and graduating first-generation college students. The Walmart Minority Student Success Initiative is a program designed to help selected minority-serving institutions (MSIs) that are already deeply committed to the academic success of first-generation, minority students to build additional capacity to serve this key group of students through faculty-driven, academic-based student success initiatives. Thirty MSIs were selected through a highly competitive application process to strengthen efforts to support first-generation students.

## PROMOTE STUDENT SUCCESS WITH GRANTS

*Minority-Serving Institutions: Doing More with Less*, a final IHEP brief in a series to disseminate the activities and findings of the Lumina MSI Models of Success project, proposes that "even beyond economy-wide trends, there is evidence to suggest that MSIs are under-resourced compared with other institutions and consequently spend relatively less per student, which may impact their ability to provide a full range of academic offerings and supports to underserved students" (p. 10).

In the context of historic underfunding and often scarce financial resources at some HBCUs, leveraging grants and external funding to help increase retention and graduation rates is one strategic approach to promote student success. HBCUs must sustain the momentum from grants and mobilize the campus community for maximum impact.

## CHAPTER 7: QUESTIONS AND NEXT STEPS

1. Outline the strategic student success ideas, research, and/or technology at the institution that could be supported or enhanced by external funding.
2. Research the potential federal, state, corporate, and not-for-profit funding opportunities available to the institution.
3. Develop a timeline for grant-proposal submission according to submission deadlines and the strategic priorities of the institution.
4. Bring campus-wide stakeholders and collaborators together to prepare grant proposals and assign duties and responsibilities for the submission of proposals.
5. How will the institution commit to sustain financial and human resources beyond the life cycle of any external grant to ensure long-term outcomes?
6. Determine how success will be measured before, during, and after each student success grant.
7. Create a methodology to correlate specific external grant and funding opportunities to discrete variances and deviations in student retention and graduation rates.

## REFERENCES

Adebola, M. (2014). NIH Awards Morgan State $23.3M Biomedical Grant. *AFRO*, October 25, 2014. Available at www.afro.com/nih-awards-morgan-state-23-3m-biomedical-grant.

Boeing, Lockheed Martin Among Top Supporters of HBCU Engineering Schools. *Diverse: Issues In Higher Education*, May 22, 2003. Available at http://diverse-education.com/article/2963.

Bryer, T. A., Augustin, M. E., Barve, M., Gracia, N., & Perez, V. (2013). Fighting Poverty with Passion and a University Partner: The Creation of a High Impact AmeriCorps VISTA Program. *Journal for Nonprofit Management*, 46.

Cunningham, A., Park, E., & Engle, J. (2014). Minority-Serving Institutions: Doing More with Less. *Institute for Higher Education Policy*. Available at www.ihep.org/research/publications/minority-serving-institutions-doing-more-less.

Franklin, K. (2014). Home Depot's Retool Your School Gives Back to HBCUs. *BlackAmericanWeb.com*. Available at http://blackamericaweb.com/2014/05/05/home-depots-melissa-brown-announces-retool-your-school-hbcu-winners.

Gasman, M. (2010). *Comprehensive Funding Approaches for Historically Black Colleges and Universities*. Available at www.gse.upenn.edu/pdf/gasman/Funding ApproachesHBCUs.pdf.

Gasman, M. (2013). Morgan State Promotes Financial Literacy. *Diverse: Issues in Higher Education*, January 2, 2013.

Hodge-Clark, K., Daniels, B. D., & the Association of Governing Boards of Universities and Colleges (2014). *Top Strategic Issues Facing HBCUs, Now and into the Future.* Washington, DC: The Association of Governing Boards of Universities and Colleges.

Journal Editors (2012). Regions Financial Enters Partnership Deal with Six HBCUs. *Journal of Blacks in Higher Education*, October 13. Available at www.jbhe.com/2012/10/regions-financial-enters-partnership-deal-with-six-hbcus.

Karp, M., & Fletcher, J. (2014). Adopting New Technologies for Student Success: A Readiness Framework. The Community College Research Center (CCRC), Teachers College, Columbia University. Available at http://ccrc.tc.columbia.edu/publications/adopting-new-technologies-for-student-success.html.

Lockheed Martin (2013). Lockheed Martin Contributes to HBCU to Foster Workforce of Tomorrow. *Diversity Best Practices*, February 21. Available at www.prnewswire.com/news-releases/lockheed-martin-contributes-to-bowie-state-university-to-foster-workforce-of-tomorrow-192267141.html.

Maryland StateStat (2013). Nearly 300 Students Back in the Classroom in First Phase of the One Step Away Program. December 7. Available at http://news.maryland.gov/statestat/2013/12/07/nearly-300-students-back-in-the-classroom-in-first-phase-of-the-one-step-away-program.

Rhodes, A. (2015). Vice President Biden Announces $25 Million in Funding for Cybersecurity Education with Focus on Minorities. *SecurityCurrent*, January 21.

Schulze, B. (2005). *Changing the Odds: Lessons Learned from the Kresge HBCU Initiative.* Troy, MI: The Kresge Foundation. Available at http://kresge.org/sites/default/files/Changing%20the%20odds_lessons%20learned.pdf.

The White House, Office of the Vice President (2015). Vice President Biden Announces $25 Million in Funding for Cybersecurity Education at HBCUs. Press Release, January 15.

## Chapter Eight

# Technology

## Tools and Systems Help
## Us Work Smarter Not Harder

One of the more common criticisms of HBCUs is the perpetual use of out-dated and/or antiquated systems and processes (Bull, Eaton & Osler, 2004; Gasman & Bowman, 2011; Britton, 2011; Fountaine, 2012). It is not uncommon to find few major changes or shifts in administrative processes on the campuses of HBCUs. This may be due in part to historic underfunding at public HBCUs, as well as the often limited financial resources at both public and private HBCUs (Gasman, 2009; Ezell & Schexnider, 2010).

Whatever the cause or historic underpinnings that may exist, now more than ever, HBCUs must catch up to and even surpass the technological efficiencies that exist in higher education today.

Chapter 7 suggests that external grant funding can serve as one major catalyst for the support of advancing technology and systems at HBCUs. While private foundations and not-for-profit organizations continue to offer opportunities to fund innovative higher education technologies, state and federal agencies offer similar opportunities for HBCUs to bring these updated systems to their institutions.

In fact, in order for HBCUs to remain competitive, it must be acknowledged that these new technologies and systems are essential and critical to the infrastructure and growth of institutions. One national study revealed the disparity of funding and resources for academic development at HBCUs compared to TWIs (traditionally white institutions) that boast greater academic development funding and resources (Kim, 2002).

Many cost-benefit analysis models will confirm that effective technology and systems actually pay for themselves over time. In 2012, an *Issues in Informing Science and Information Technology* article proposed a specific framework to make it possible to use the cost-benefit analysis model to help colleges and universities with determining the feasibility (or lack of it) of investing in software upgrades (Ali, 2012). The author submits that "an academic program with superior technology is able to fulfill the latest demand better than others with older technology" (p. 407).

Updating outdated and antiquated systems helps to facilitate efficiency, leading to higher productivity and ultimately to success that can be measured by specific outcomes at the institution. In other words, these innovative tools can promote student success and degree completion by enabling administrators, faculty, staff, and students to work smarter and not necessarily harder. And these tools do not seek to replace human engagement and interaction at institutions of higher learning, but rather to facilitate it in the most resourceful and effective ways.

This chapter details the implementation of several new technologies and tools that have promoted student success and retention at Morgan State University including Google Apps (Google's Gmail, Google Drive, Google Calendar, etc.), Starfish Retention Solutions, and Degree Works™ by Ellucian. It further introduces existing tools at Morgan such as Blackboard, Oracle APEX, Campus Labs, and Smarthinking. It concludes by highlighting several other new and innovative student success and retention technologies including tools by Civitas Learning™, Hobsons, and GradesFirst.


## THE FOUNDATION: A STUDENT INFORMATION SYSTEM

The Banner student information system (SIS) by Ellucian provides the means for a university to function as an integrated system, sharing one database, with departments working together systematically to serve the student population. Banner is a web-based, administrative software application managed by Ellucian specifically for higher education institutions. Whether it is the university calendar or student registration, the SIS can incorporate each school, department, and program into the establishment of policy, the development of procedures, or the setting of deadlines.

At Morgan, each major department has one individual assigned to serve as the data custodian responsible for deciding a user's level of Banner access for navigation and reporting purposes. Self-Service Banner, known as WebSIS, is a user-friendly online tool that allows for management of personal and academic information through the use of hyperlinks, eliminating the need to stand in line or fill out paper forms. One researcher suggests that data custodians and users at colleges and universities actually become emotionally attached to these processes and systems, even if they can be proven to be inefficient or cumbersome (Buche, 2013).

## A SMOOTH SWITCH TO GOOGLE

In 2011, Morgan changed its email platform to Google for faculty, staff, and students. Thanks to the support of numerous departments and a strong communications campaign, the institution was able to successfully complete the email-conversion project with minimal bumps along the way. For instance, partnerships with several student organizations, residence-life staff, honors staff, computer lab managers, and the school newspaper staff helped communicate the upcoming changes and the impact that the Google Apps suite would have on email usage and retrieval.

The university hosted an all-day, one-on-one workshop in the student center to provide faculty, staff, and students with face-to-face guidance through the conversion process. Trainings were made available both in person and online. Tutorials, user guides, and FAQs were published online to assist those who required additional support.

There were two major attitudes and/or behaviors that Morgan's IT team discovered that promoted efforts to implement the Google Apps suite and its functionalities: (1) an open mind about and willingness to change current processes; and (2) end-user motivation to embrace the product and begin using it right away.

## IPAS: A NEW ACRONYM

Morgan State University's Office of Student Success and Retention (OSSR) applied for and was awarded a $100,000 grant from the Bill & Melinda Gates Foundation for the implementation of Integrated Planning and Advising Services (IPAS) technology. After initial meetings with and demonstrations from Blackboard, Ellucian, Campus Labs, and Starfish Retention Solutions, Morgan identified Starfish as its designated IPAS system for implementation by spring 2014. Starfish assists Morgan in two focused areas: counseling and coaching, and risk targeting and intervention.

OSSR staff spend most of their time monitoring and tracking students' finances and satisfactory academic progress. Initially using only Microsoft Excel, Oracle Application Express (APEX), and Google Docs, each semester OSSR staff track and systematically monitor students. Because OSSR staff were working as academic coaches and counselors already, and targeting students for strategic interventions based on cohort designations, Starfish was an ideal partner to assist and facilitate Morgan in using IPAS technology to go to the next level.

The many hours it took OSSR staff to identify students using minimal technology and manual cross referencing, contact students individually by email and phone, and report data both manually and individually in a Google document have been dramatically decreased with the help of IPAS technology provided by Starfish Retention Solutions.

The OSSR has become more efficient and more effective in its efforts. Campus constituents including students, faculty, and OSSR advisors have greatly benefited from IPAS technology. Students, for the first time, have one portal to view all of their faculty, mentors, and advisors' outreach efforts and recommendations.

Faculty, with little change to their current workload, are able to trigger early alerts for students in their courses with just one screen-shot per class, and are able to see who on campus has followed up on their early alert(s); fittingly, faculty now have the ability to distinguish which students have accessed resources on campus such as academic support, mentoring, or tutoring as a result of their early alert(s).

OSSR advisors no longer manually identify students in a "vacuum," but rather access information through Starfish to identify, track, advise, and intervene with students in a way that is transparent to students, faculty, and other campus constituents. Simply put, Starfish has revolutionized Morgan's student success and retention processes!

Starfish has been an ideal partner to assist and facilitate Morgan's using IPAS technology to go to the next level. The goals of Morgan's IPAS implementation and adoption were: (1) to increase faculty-triggered early alerts; (2) to increase students' utilization of campus resources; (3) to provide seamless, transparent, and user-friendly monitoring and tracking of students in high-risk cohorts; and (4) to provide one online resource where faculty, staff, and students can access feedback and action plans for student success.

## IPAS BENEFITS AND OUTCOMES

IPAS technology and its functionalities have provided Morgan State University with an integrated tracking and advising system that is meeting the needs of and improving communication among different campus constituents. Thus far, IPAS has motivated university employees to work harmoniously toward establishing and enforcing consistent, collaborative, university-wide retention and advising practices.

The potential benefits of the IPAS system are in line with the university's goal to improve retention and degree-completion rates by enhancing programs and practices and by identifying and implementing national best practices shown to improve retention and graduation among graduate and undergraduate students.

Morgan State University anticipates long-term IPAS adoption success as measured by several key outcomes. At the institutional level, it is expected that IPAS implementation will result in higher retention at the freshman to sophomore level and less attrition from the second to third year, where the highest dropout/stop-out rate is observed. Also, it is anticipated that Starfish will facilitate long-term increased volume in student visits to campus support offices such as the Counseling Center, the Career Development Center, the Center for Academic Success and Achievement, the Writing Center, the Student Disabilities Support Services Office, the OSSR, and the Academic Enrichment Program.

Since Starfish Retention Solutions provides an online virtual check-in and virtual waiting room for every office on campus, as well as the ability for students to schedule appointments for any campus office from their computer, tablet or smartphone, increased volume in scheduled appointments and in-person visits is greatly anticipated.

For instructional faculty, the most anticipated outcome is an increase in early alerts initiated by faculty. And, as a result of those early alerts, it is expected that over time D, W, I, and F grades will decrease at midterm and finals. Because Starfish is very user friendly, Morgan faculty have embraced the new technology and participate in early alert and intervention systems throughout the semester.

For the OSSR staff (advising, coaching, and counseling staff), it is expected that Starfish will continue to reduce the hours of time spent identifying cohorts of students to be contacted manually. Also, it is expected that Starfish will allow for ongoing, seamless intervention by the OSSR staff for identified cohorts of students, especially the early alerts triggered by instructional faculty. The result has been automated, individualized email and text messages to students from OSSR staff.

For students, Starfish provides access to one online resource where all academic coaching and mentoring as initiated by OSSR staff, academic advisors, and faculty can be obtained and acted on. It is expected that students' response rates to interventions including the scheduling of appointments will continue to increase and facilitate more engagement with faculty, staff, and student support offices.

## TRANSITION AND BUY-IN

The OSSR has served as the lead department for IPAS implementation and adoption. OSSR staff were trained by Starfish consultants to train Morgan faculty, students, and other staff in various offices on campus. The OSSR has worked closely with IT on all technical components of IPAS adoption. OSSR staff already were a well-organized staff capable of executing systematic intervention for students without IPAS technology; with IPAS technology, OSSR staff have become more efficient and available to students for in-person coaching and mentoring.

To ensure buy-in, the Office of the Provost and Vice President for Academic Affairs introduced faculty to Starfish during the mandatory Faculty Institute in August 2013. Faculty and staff were trained by OSSR staff during the spring 2014 semester. New students were introduced to Starfish during summer 2014 orientation programs for freshmen and transfer students. Continuing students were introduced to Starfish by faculty in their spring 2014 courses as well as through campus announcements and social media inviting students to view online YouTube videos. Access to Starfish is granted via Blackboard and Self-Service Banner (WebSIS).

Challenges included integration of Starfish into existing technologies such as Blackboard and Banner. However, Morgan's IT staff were committed to ensuring full IPAS integration and adoption by the spring 2014 semester. Because Starfish boasts more than two hundred clients, many of whom use Blackboard and Banner, Starfish remained confident that full adoption at Morgan was indeed possible within six months. Otherwise, training with limited time and allowing time for OSSR staff to train faculty and staff were a concern as well. With the support and enthusiasm of President David Wilson and Morgan's provost, buy-in for faculty and staff was inevitable.

A May 2014 convening of the Bill & Melinda Gates IPAS institutions yielded three important lessons:

1. Good technical implementation must be accompanied by good process implementations;
2. Implementing an IPAS system inevitably requires excellent change-management leadership;
3. There's a lot of noise around consolidating technologies, but little action so far. (Enit, 2014)

According to Enit, IPAS technology represents a rapidly evolving market for better student-support technology platforms and aligned business processes.

# CHANGE MANAGEMENT

The adoption of any new technology on a college campus should be preceded by a number of strategic steps to foster success. When I wrote the Bill & Melinda Gates Foundation IPAS grant to obtain Starfish Retention Solutions as our vendor partner, I knew that a campus-wide adoption would require partnerships and collaboration across campus. However, I also knew that those partnerships and collaborations would not be enough to drive the adoption and implementation for all faculty, staff, and students, especially over the timeframe of one academic year.

No matter how much collaboration there is on campus to drive the adoption of a new technology, if you ask most faculty and staff, "do you want to learn a new software or technology?" the answer may not be positive. In a culture where faculty and staff do more with much less than their counterparts at TWIs, often teaching more students each semester without the assistance of teaching assistants and mentoring students on an individual basis, while still meeting the research and publication standards of an institution, trying to encourage buy-in is often a dead-end street.

Few people will volunteer to add more to their already full plate. Selecting technology, software, and tools that will help faculty and staff to work smarter and be more effective is the fundamental ingredient in driving culture change. If the right people, both the end-users and the leadership who understand the larger vision, are involved from the beginning in selecting new technologies, software, and tools that are highly effective and user friendly, culture change will be the byproduct of campus-wide adoption.

So instead of asking who wants to learn a new software or technology, campus leaders, partners, and collaborators should simply bring a new technology solution to the campus with sufficient training and adequate support for faculty, staff, and students with the confidence that this new tool will "win people over" on its own merits. Much time can be wasted when administrators try to solicit buy-in for a new technology instead of just moving forward with an implementation with the support of campus leadership, collaborators, and partners.

Our IPAS/Starfish implementation was successful because we had the right people, supported by our senior leadership, guide the campus through a campus-wide adoption that was not presented as an option, but rather as an effective solution that everyone would participate in and have the opportunity to evaluate and give feedback about its effectiveness.

## A USER-FRIENDLY TOOL

One of the selling points for Starfish has been the extreme ease of use for faculty, staff, and students. The Starfish platform is inviting and engaging; once end-users access the IPAS system, they love and appreciate its ease of use. A number of emails and phone calls have been received from students and faculty expressing thanks and positive feedback for Starfish.

One of the senior faculty on Morgan's IPAS Advisory Committee in the Department of Psychology couldn't wait to give a positive report during a University Assessment Committee meeting. She said that after weeks of trying to get her students' attention in her four psychology courses, she completed the first progress survey in Starfish during the previous week before the committee meeting and immediately, right after she clicked "submit," students began to email her. Because every flag in Starfish generates a personalized email sent from the flag raiser's email address, typically from an instructor, when students reply to the email it comes to the inbox of the instructor.

The senior faculty member could not believe that students were immediately responsive, so quickly. Could engaging and captivating students' attention be as simple as to send students personalized emails from their faculty identifying specific behaviors in their courses such as class attendance, participation, and missing assignments that they instantly respond to? The senior faculty member reported more email responses, in-person appointments, and students returning to her classes after completing her progress surveys in Starfish than any other semester in her forty years of teaching in higher education. She said that if she could use Starfish, and love it, and believe in its merits, anyone can!

## THE RESULTS ARE IN. . . .

After conducting sixteen two-hour faculty/staff trainings with more than 275 participants, Morgan launched its campus-wide Starfish initiative in March 2014. By February 2015, after two semesters of implementation, there were 63,223 Starfish flags (tracking items) including 23,683 flags from progress surveys, 17,052 system-raised midterm grade flags, 9,818 system-raised final grade flags, 3,171 system-raised high-priority student flags, 2,261 system-raised GPA<2.0 flags, 5,203 kudos, 485 referrals or to do's, and 1,550 manually raised flags by instructors in Starfish. Additionally, 39,110 attendance records were taken by faculty, 3,968 profiles were created and/or updated, 729 faculty/advisor office hour schedules were added, and 2,563 appointments were made, updated, and/or canceled in Starfish between March 2014 and February 2015.

The implementation of Starfish exceeded expectations! Campus-wide buy-in and excitement were progressive. Faculty/staff and student surveys were developed to assess perception and culture change; surveys were deployed by email in December 2014 and were to be evaluated during the spring 2015 semester. Faculty members on Morgan's IPAS Advisory Committee designed comprehensive, system-level evaluation models to include tracking associations and correlations between flags raised in Starfish and final grades, results in courses where progress surveys were completed versus results in courses where progress surveys were not completed, comparing course outcomes from a current semester to course outcomes from previous semesters, and so on.

## MANUAL DEGREE AUDITING

In 2014, Morgan proposed to invest in much-needed degree-auditing software, Degree Works™ by Ellucian, to promote degree completion for near-completers. With four years of experience with near-completers (see chapter 6 for a detailed discussion on near-completers), the one consistent challenge has been obtaining an official degree audit and an "exit strategy" for students attempting to re-enroll. Prior to 2015, Morgan used 100 percent manual degree auditing in each academic department, school, and college. Individuals (evaluators) used a variety of hard-copy forms developed in their departments to evaluate students' progress in their degree program.

Typically, students were given a hard-copy degree plan as freshmen, and carried it around with them for the next four, five, or six years. Multiple copies of this hard-copy form were made every time students met with their academic advisor. Finally, when students applied for graduation, an "official" senior credit audit was requested by the Office of Records and Registration from the dean and/or chairperson of students' departments. The designated official (evaluator) in the school or department used another hard-copy form to evaluate the students' transcripts in Banner and determine their eligibility for graduation, as well as their status in their academic program. This was a long, detailed, and tedious process for the evaluator, as well as for the students and advisors waiting to obtain the official degree audit.

While working with Morgan's near-completers who were attempting to re-enroll at the university, the most challenging issue had been the obtaining of official degree audits from a department, school, or college. The Reclamation Initiative program director had to write memos and "official" emails to request degree audits for each near-completer and include a justification for each request. Except for the initial hard copy of students' four-year degree plan that they received from their academic advisor in their first year, students had no way of knowing their status in their degree program on a semester-by-semester basis.

This was especially difficult for stop-out students and near-completers. Many times their degree program had changed or had been modified in terms of course requirements. Waiting for an official degree audit can delay students' time to graduation and create a sense of unnecessary frustration. Best practices suggest that students should always know and/or have access to their status in their degree program.

That is why Morgan took one "giant" step toward long-term success by using the Maryland One Step Away grant for near-completers to invest in much-needed degree-auditing software, Degree Works™ by Ellucian, to assist near-completers and all undergraduate students in obtaining their official degree audit and an "exit strategy" for degree completion.

Complete College America has identified Guided Pathways to Success (GPS) as one of five "game-changer" strategies to promote college completion.

> Guided Pathways to Success (GPS) enabled by technology, default all students into highly structured degree plans, not individual courses. Start students in a limited number of "meta majors," which narrow into majors. Map out every semester of study for the entire program, and guarantee that milestone courses will be available when needed. Use built-in early warning systems to alert advisers when students fall behind to ensure efficient intervention. (Complete College America, 2014)

## WHY DEGREE-AUDITING SOFTWARE?

The benefits of investing in degree-auditing software are:

1. enabling the institution to accelerate degree-audit approvals;
2. improving the overall quality of students'/near-completers' experience through user-friendly on-demand features such as degree shopping; and
3. providing a robust, scalable, and configurable campus-wide solution that meets all requirements of the degree-auditing process.

Additional long-term benefits of degree-auditing software include:

- students not wasting time and money on unnecessary courses;
- reducing students' stress level about graduating on time;
- providing advisors and evaluators with more time to provide insightful advice that supports better student outcomes;

- monitoring course demand and offering the right classes at the right time for near-completers; and
- integrating the software with the SIS so that interactions with students are recorded so deans, chairs, and advisors can see what students see as far as degree monitoring and degree shopping.

Degree shopping enables students to compare their progress in one degree program or major field of study at the institution to other degree programs or major fields of study at the institution so that students can make informed decisions as to how to progress and persist toward degree completion.

The following technologies, tools, and systems are available to promote student success and degree completion at HBCUs.

## GOOGLE APPS

Google Apps (www.google.com/work/apps/education) is a cloud-based messaging and collaboration platform that includes mail, calendaring, IM, as well as web-based collaborative documents, spreadsheets, presentations, and sites. Google Apps for Education is helping schools offer their communities better ways of working together, with over 14 million students, faculty, and staff worldwide now using Google Apps for Education and seventy-two of the top one hundred universities in the United States having gone Google (Sheepdog, 2014).

More and more institutions for higher education are using the cloud to improve collaboration, increase efficiency, save costs, and reduce environmental impact without sacrificing privacy or security. Herrick concluded in 2009 that "the integration of other Google Apps services, such as Calendar, Talk, Docs and Sites, has been a great boon to Google Apps users' collaboration and productivity" (p. 64).

Additionally, data collected in a 2010 study from both in-depth customer interviews and broader customer surveys demonstrates that migrating an organization's messaging and collaboration environment from legacy on-premise systems to Google Apps has the potential to provide a solid return on the investment (Erickson & Van Metre, 2010).

## STARFISH RETENTION SOLUTIONS

The Starfish platform (www.starfishsolutions.com) helps eliminate the silos that make it difficult to share the information that could impact a student's ability to be successful. The platform provides an easy way to collect data from the people and systems that are working at the institution; Starfish provides that information to advisors and other staff at the right time to initiate and document a plan of action. Starfish provides simple tools to create efficiencies and allow an institution to scale its student success programs, either by making services available to more students or by engaging specific students in a deeper way (Starfish, 2015).

Starfish Retention Solutions outlines five "G's" that can help make student success resolutions become reality:

1. Get Key Players Involved (faculty, enrollment management, academic and student services, IR, and IT);
2. Gather Information (data in student information systems, learning-management systems, and other campus data);
3. Go for SMART Goals (Specific, Measurable, Assignable, Realistic, and Time related);
4. Give Implementation, Evaluation, and Communication Planning Importance; and
5. Generate Grit (improve the outcomes of students).

Authors at East Carolina University (Faulconer, Geissler, Majewski & Trifilo, 2014) have found that:

> initial data support the notion that this technology tool (Starfish) has the potential to create a more cohesive approach to monitoring the academic progress of university students. In addition, early evidence suggests an early-alert system has the potential to impact student success by enhancing in real time the lines of communication among student, instructor, and advisor. (p. 48)

## DEGREE WORKS™ BY ELLUCIAN

Ellucian's Degree Works™ (www.ellucian.com/Software/Ellucian-Degree-Works) is a comprehensive academic advising, transfer articulation, and degree-audit solution that aligns students, advisors, and institutions to a common goal: helping students graduate on time. Degree Works™ helps students stay motivated and graduate on time by encouraging them to reach goals, providing support to advisors, monitoring course demand and offering the right classes at the right time, and increasing enrollment by simplifying transfer articulation. One doctoral dissertation has found that:

> after administrating gap analysis surveys of the current Degree Audit (DA) system, user tests of the VDA (Degree Works™), and comparing the results of the

post evaluation surveys, it has been suggested that the VDA (Degree Works™) is successful in decreasing the student learning curve while increasing students' knowledge, efficiency, and personal control over their higher education journey. It (Degree Works™) was able to provide a comprehensive resource application for students to access the information they need to plan their degrees in one place. (Hom-Nici, 2014, p. 82)

## BLACKBOARD

Blackboard (www.blackboard.com) aims to assist in the delivery of higher education by driving targeted growth to achieve enrollment goals, increasing enrollments and improving overall student satisfaction by meeting the rising expectations of students, faculty, and staff, and improving the student experience with a learning environment that extends beyond the classroom. Blackboard's goal is to make learning more desirable, accessible, and meaningful for learners. Out of the Top 50 Times Higher Education Reputation Ranking in 2014, 80 percent of the world's top academic institutions work with Blackboard. Aside from Google, Blackboard claims to be the number one website that college students can't live without.

According to Blackboard, one of the best ways to reach today's active, tech-savvy students is to deliver learning where students already are: on smartphones and tablets. Blackboard lists five reasons to choose Blackboard and to go mobile:

1. Develop a secure, user-friendly mobile platform.
2. Help students get to campus and to class on time.
3. Leverage push notifications to keep students informed.
4. Bring high-tech educational experiences to mobile devices.
5. Meet the unique needs of the college or university.

Blackboard Mobile Learn extends the experience of the online learning-management system, Blackboard Learn, onto mobile devices; Blackboard Mobile Central is a suite of features in a single mobile application that provides campus-life resources and information—like student and faculty directories, news, brick-and-mortar campus maps, dining menus, and more—on mobile devices.

## ORACLE

Oracle Application Express (Oracle APEX, https://apex.oracle.com/i) is Oracle's primary tool for developing web applications with SQL and PL/

SQL. Oracle APEX facilitates the development and deployment of professional web-based applications for desktops and mobile devices using only a web browser. At Morgan State University, APEX is used across campus and in departments to help build and maintain database-driven applications on the web to provide users with a very easy-to-use web-based environment for reporting and tracking.

Morgan currently hosts a number of APEX applications in the production environment for departments including information technology, institutional research, the Office of the Provost, the Office of Residence Life, the Office of Admission and Recruitment, the OSSR, and the academic schools/colleges. APEX reporting has been an essential component of the "case-management" approach to systematically track and monitor undergraduate students at Morgan State University.

## CAMPUS LABS

In partnership with the Council for the Advancement of Standards in Higher Education, the Higher Learning Commission, Student Affairs Administrators in Higher Education (NASPA), the Network for Campus Engagement, and EverFi, Campus Labs (www.campuslabs.com) is working to promote the use of data, assessment, and self-study for the continued development of quality programs and services across all elements of higher education. Each partnership is based on Campus Labs' commitment to creating a new segment in educational technology: the centralized repository for all meaningful data and performance analytics in higher education, something Campus Labs calls "Campus Intelligence."

Campus Labs (formerly known as Student Voice) has become a leading platform and service provider for assessment in higher education. Campus Labs is a specialized, comprehensive assessment program that combines data collection, reporting, organization, and campus-wide integration.

Through its partnership with the NASPA Assessment & Knowledge Consortium, Campus Labs offers participating campuses benchmark assessments to administer during an academic year based on campus priorities. These consortium studies are designed to provide colleges and universities with actionable campus-specific and benchmarking data to shape and enhance programming inside and outside the classroom.

## SMARTHINKING

Smarthinking (www.smarthinking.com) is a provider of research-based online tutoring to help institutions of higher education increase student achievement, boost retention, and enhance learning. More than one thousand colleges and universities use Smarthinking's services every year. Smarthinking offers students online tutoring that is available twenty-four hours a day, seven days a week, enabling students to get the help they need when they need it. Through Smarthinking students connect to live educators from any computer that has internet access, with no special software installation or equipment required.

Findings of one longitudinal study conclude that students and tutors perceive a value from the guidance received through the Smarthinking online writing lab, and that there was a positive correlation and impact on retention, completion, and grades achieved by students who used the Smarthinking online writing lab compared to peers who did not (De Fazio & Crock, 2008). Results from 2000 report indicate that:

1. students reacted positively to the program and would utilize it in the future;
2. instructors were positive but noncommittal about utilizing the program and offered several improvement suggestions;
3. Smarthinking does not coincide with the interpersonal interaction characteristic of the writing center. (Moe, p. 1)

## CIVITAS LEARNING™

By building a community of forward-thinking higher education institutions, Civitas Learning™ (www.civitaslearning.com) brings together new technology, design thinking, and data science in its mission to help a million more college students learn well and finish strong. Using a cloud-based, predictive analytics platform and engaging applications, Civitas Learning helps partner institutions bring deep insights to decision makers, and personalized, real-time recommendations directly to the frontlines for students, faculty, and advisors to measurably improve student learning, persistence, and graduation.

Civitas Learning serves more than thirty-five partner institutions and systems in higher education that enroll more than 1.3 million students. The historical data set from these partners currently includes more than 10 million students and 100 million enrollment records. "Civitas leverages digital tools students use to compose their holistic story from their digital footprint. This data helps schools create scalable, predictive flow models that are updated on a regular basis" (Harven, 2014).

## HOBSONS

Hobsons (www.hobsons.com) solutions allow students to develop personalized academic and career plans based on their goals, interests, abilities, and learning styles. Used by more than two thousand institutions, Hobsons' college software helps admissions and enrollment professionals reach and connect with students that are the right fit for their institutions while enabling retention professionals to help students stay on track so they achieve their goals.

Hobsons' admissions software and marketing solutions help streamline the communication, application, and enrollment process so institutions can engage with the right students at the right time through the right channels. Hobsons' *Agilegrad* solution provides insight into each student's plan, allowing institutions to review, alter, and monitor a student's course load and path to graduation.

## GRADESFIRST

GradesFirst (http://gradesfirst.com) technology combines early alert, advising-management, integrated communications, and tutoring-management services, maximizing the impact of quality academic advising. The components of GradesFirst's Comprehensive Student Success Solution are: Advising Management—Streamline advisor workflow, leaving more room for student engagement and retention; Tutoring Management—Maximize tutoring investment, reinforcing academic discipline and increasing student success; Predictive Analytics; Early Alert—Ensure all students who are performing poorly are identified as at risk before it's too late; Conversations—Empower campus support staff with optimized and secure tools for student communication; and Athletics—Monitor academic progress and ensure student-athletes maintain eligibility.

## CHAPTER 8: QUESTIONS AND NEXT STEPS

1. What are the current technologies, software, and/or tools utilized at the institution to promote student success, and are they up to date with the latest version(s)?
2. Collect survey data from the current users of the existing technologies, software, and/or tools to inform potential upgrades and future decisions.
3. Are there any manual, outdated, or antiquated systems or processes that need to be changed or enhanced?

4. Research current technologies, software, and/or tools by viewing online videos, hosting demonstrations, and/or contacting peer institutions who are clients of or partners with potential vendors and solution providers.
5. Determine what technologies, software, and/or tools will advance the strategic student success goals of the institution.
6. Conduct a cost-benefit analysis for each technology, software, and/or tool to analyze the feasibility of adoption and implementation.
7. Identify the stakeholders, collaborators, and partners at the institution to involve in the adoption of each technology, software, and/or tool and develop a change-management strategy.

## REFERENCES

Ali, A. (2012). A Framework for Using Cost-Benefit Analysis in Making the Case for Software Upgrade. *Issues in Informing Science & Information Technology, 9,* 399.

Britton, D. (2011). HBCU Blues: America's Historically Black Colleges and Universities in the 21st Century. *Huffington Post,* August 29. Available at www.huffington post.com/della-britton/hbcu-funding-_b_938550.html.

Buche, M. W. (2013). The Elimination of Detrimental Shadow Systems: A Participant Observer Case Study. MWAIS 2013 Proceedings, paper 1.

Bull, P., Eaton, D., & Osler, J. (2004). Faculty Technology Development and Integration: Perceptions of HBCU School of Education Faculty to Technology Integration and Faculty Technology Development. In Society for Information Technology and Teacher Education International Conference and Association for the Advancement of Computing in Education, *Society for Information Technology & Teacher Education International Conference* (vol. 2004, no. 1, pp. 1986–91). Chesapeake, VA: Association for the Advancement of Computing in Education.

Complete College America (2014). The Game Changers. Available at http://completecollege.org/the-game-changers.

De Fazio, T., & Crock, M. (2008, November). Enabling Learning, Addressing Retention: Supporting Students via Online Tutorials with Smarthinking. ASCILITE Conference Proceedings, Melbourne, Australia. Available at www.ascilite.org.au/conferences/melbourne08/procs/defazio-2.pdf.

Ellucian (2015). Ellucian Degree Works. Available at www.ellucian.com/Solutions/Ellucian-Degree-Works.

Enit, V. (2014). 3 Lessons from the Gates Foundation's 2014 IPAS Meeting. *Student Success Insights Blog.* Education Advisory Board. Available at www.eab.com/technology/student-success-collaborative/student-success-insights/2014/05/three-lessons-from-the-gates-foundation-2014-ipas-meeting.

Erickson, J., & Van Metre, E. (2010). *Measuring the Total Economic Impact of Google Apps: A Cross-Industry Survey and Analysis.* A Forrester Total Economic Impact™ Study Prepared for Google.

*Chapter Eight*

Ezell, J. L., & Schexnider, A. J. (2010). Leadership, Governance and Sustainability of Black Colleges and Universities. *Trusteeship, 18*(3), 25–28.

Faulconer, J., Geissler, J., Majewski, D., & Trifilo, J. (2014). Adoption of an Early-Alert System to Support University Student Success. *Delta Kappa Gamma Bulletin, 80*(2), 45–48.

Fountaine, T. P. (2012). Black Graduate Education at Historically Black Colleges and Universities. *Black Graduate Education at Historically Black Colleges and Universities: Trends, Experiences, and Outcomes*, 11.

Gasman, M. (2009). Historically Black Colleges and Universities in a Time of Economic Crisis. *Academe, 95*(6), 26–28.

Gasman, M., & Bowman III, N. (2011). How to Paint a Better Portrait of HBCUs. *Academe, 97*(3), 24–27.

Harven, M. (2014). Edtech Startups Using Big Data: Civitas. *EdTech Times*, September 30. Available at http://edtechtimes.com/2014/09/30/edtech-startups-using-big-data-civitas.

Herrick, D. R. (2009, October). Google This!: Using Google Apps for Collaboration and Productivity. In *Proceedings of the 37th Annual ACM SIGUCCS Fall Conference: Communication and Collaboration* (pp. 55–64). New York: ACM.

Hom-Nici, E. (2014). Design and Construction of Visual Degree Audit Software: An Application of Visual Communication, Project Management, and Graph Theory. Doctoral dissertation, Texas State University–San Marcos.

Kim, M. M. (2002). Historically Black vs. White Institutions: Academic Development among Black Students. *Review of Higher Education, 25*(4), 385–407.

Moe, H. K. (2000). *Smarthinking.com—Online Writing Lab or Jiffy-Editing Service?* ERIC Database. Available at http://eric.ed.gov/?id=ED440383.

Sheepdog: People Not Seats (2014). *Top 5 Advantages of Google Apps for Higher Education.* Available at https://s3.amazonaws.com/sheepdog-website/Whitepaper-Top_5_Advantages_of_Google_Apps_for_Higher_Education.pdf.

Starfish Retention Solutions (2015). Starfish Early Alert [Software]. Arlington, VA: Starfish Retention Solutions. Available at www.starfishsolutions.com.

# Chapter Nine

# Networking

## *Documenting and Sharing Your Successes and Failures*

In a professional climate where resources are often scarce, allocating funding to support strategic priorities is never easy. Professional development for faculty, staff, and administrators may fall to the bottom of the list when more pressing issues such as performance-based funding, accreditation status, research and grants, and student learning outcomes dominate and demand the attention of the institution's senior leadership. However, networking with colleagues and documenting the successes and failures of the institution should not be neglected, especially not at HBCUs.

One definition of *professional development* (academic development, or educational development, or staff development) is the development, self-development, and institutional management of faculty or academic staff at all levels with reference to their activities and responsibilities as teachers and managers in higher education (Zuber-Skerritt, 1994).

Another author outlined four types of attitudes toward professional development: staff who do not want or endorse professional development for themselves or for their colleagues, staff who do not want or endorse professional development for themselves but tolerate it for others, staff who express enthusiasm for some professional development but do not participate in it, and staff who actively engage in professional development (Roe, 1986).

Developing administrators, faculty, and staff regardless of their attitudes toward professional development can be challenging. Nevertheless, it must be recognized that change is inevitable and that professional development can help prepare the higher education community of educators and practitioners to meet change, head-on, with renewed vigor, best practices, and innovation.

Professional development, both formal and informal, is one component of learning for higher education practitioners who understand the need to change and who understand that change involves continual learning (Nicholls, 2014).

## BEING THE ONLY HBCU TO ATTEND . . .

In 2007, when a decision was made at Morgan to move the new-student orientation program for freshmen from another office on campus to the Office of Student Retention, I began to search online for resources to help me restructure and enhance the program.

I soon discovered an association dedicated to the study of new-student orientation, the National Orientation Directors Association (NODA), now known as the Association for Orientation, Transition, and Retention in Higher Education. I quickly made plans for me and a retention coordinator to attend the upcoming national conference.

The conference was much larger than we expected with more than 1,500 attendees. There were dozens of informative breakout sessions to choose from over the duration of the four-day conference. We both participated in OPI, Orientation Professionals Institute, an annual pre-conference training program specifically designed to educate new orientation staff and administrators.

I sat down with my staff member, and we planned how we would maximize our time at the conference. We met daily before and/or after plenary sessions to swap notes. What became obvious to us was the absence of any other HBCU representatives at the conference. Although there was vast diversity in terms of institution type, institution size, institutional regions and locations, and types of attendees (administrators, staff, and students), we were the only HBCU represented that year.

In my years of active participation in NODA since 2008, I have been successful in recommending targeted sessions specifically geared toward HBCUs. One of the benefits of this particular conference, National Orientation Directors Association Conference (NODAC), is the exchange of data through national benchmarking.

As a result of my attendance to this annual conference, Morgan has participated in three biannual national student orientation benchmark surveys. Regrettably, we are the only HBCU listed among the benchmark institutions each year. The absence of HBCUs at NODAC is perpetuated by the lack of participation in the benchmark study as well.

Attending NODAC each year is a significant investment of time and financial resources; however, I have been able to utilize the benchmarking data in decision-making processes to continue to improve and strengthen the new-student orientation program at Morgan, and OPI has become my official training program for each new program coordinator for freshman orientation.

## NO NEED TO "REINVENT THE WHEEL"

Arguably, the greatest benefit of attending conferences for the purpose of professional development is the exchange of ideas among colleagues. "Trial and error" is one approach to launching new programs and initiatives; however, learning from the successes and failures of peers can prevent wasted time, lost money, and squandered buy-in at the institution.

The results of one study of Student Affairs administrators at HBCUs suggest that the pace of work is positively challenging and highly stressful and that change is slow to be adopted (Hirt, Strayhorn, Amelink & Bennett, 2006). The authors recommend that graduate faculty consider developing graduate students through workshops and/or courses on how to manage stress and promote change within organizations.

There is no need to "reinvent the wheel" when similar institutions have piloted programs and initiatives on their campuses and lessons have been learned. Even though no two colleges or universities are the same, certain similarities may exist that permit comparisons in strategy and approach. Moreover, shared conclusions and recommendations from peer institutions at least can contribute to the decision-making process by providing context and perspective.

## GETTING THE "REAL DEAL" FROM COLLEAGUES

In 2013 when an opportunity to apply for a Bill & Melinda Gates Foundation grant presented itself to my associate provost, and she mandated that I apply for the grant, I attended the 16th Annual HBCU Summit on Retention in Ocean City, MD. I have served on the Steering Committee for this conference for a number of years, and I look forward to the exchange of ideas with my colleagues in the region annually.

This particular year, a colleague at Bowie State University, one of the other public HBCUs in the state of Maryland, asked if I wouldn't mind sitting down with him and his staff to discuss some ideas that they had for restructuring their retention program based on a model that we already had implemented at Morgan.

I was thrilled to accept his invitation for a "sit-down," especially because I knew that Bowie already was a client of Starfish Retention Solutions, my proposed vendor partner for the Bill & Melinda Gates

Foundation grant that I had just submitted the week before the summit in Ocean City. I spent several hours with the student success team at Bowie exchanging ideas and lessons learned. I shared our retention model with them, and they shared their Starfish experience with me.

The results of this one meeting were exponential! Because of their guidance and open dialogue about their experience with Starfish, I came into my new grant empowered with information from my colleagues that positively impacted our implementation schedule, our integration preference, and our customizable features in Starfish. Our Starfish implementation was an overwhelming success, and Bowie's new retention model is now three years in the making.

Because this particular conference, the Regional HBCU Summit on Retention, attracts just over two hundred attendees annually, one-on-one interaction and engagement are fostered and encouraged. I always walk away from this conference with new insights from my colleagues regarding what is "the real deal" on their campuses as I reciprocate by sharing with them our successes and challenges at Morgan.

## WHY ATTEND CONFERENCES?

Participation in global, national, and regional conferences and workshops offers myriad benefits for higher education professionals including networking with colleagues, exchanging ideas with peers, building the curriculum vitae, staying current with new tools and technologies, and anticipating trends in higher education.

Not only do professional development and participation in conferences act as a tool for higher education administrators by fostering dialogue with peers on best practices, but professional development also can increase job satisfaction levels of administrators where low morale, stress, and limited resources can help to foster premature career exits and/or transitions (Jackson, 2001).

Listed in the balance of this chapter are just some of the relevant organizations and the professional-development opportunities that are offered to promote increased retention and graduation rates. More detailed information can be obtained from their websites (as listed) or by contacting the organization directly.

## THE WHITE HOUSE INITIATIVE ON HISTORICALLY BLACK COLLEGES AND UNIVERSITIES

The Annual National Historically Black Colleges and Universities Week Conference is planned under the leadership of the White House Initiative on HBCUs (www.ed.gov/edblogs/whhbcu) and with input from the President's Board of Advisors on HBCUs and its conference sponsors. It provides a forum to exchange information and share innovations among and between institutions. Stakeholders—which include federal agencies, private-sector companies, and philanthropic organizations—provide an overview of successful engagements that if replicated may improve instruction, degree completion, and the understanding of federal policies that shape and support higher education.

The Annual National HBCUs Week Conference is usually held in September and features five tracks:

1. the Executive Session (by invitation only) for HBCU presidents and chancellors, foundation executives, and senior federal officials;
2. the Research and Institutional Advancement track for vice presidents for research and development, vice presidents for institutional advancement, sponsored programs directors, and faculty;
3. the Academic Affairs and Faculty Development track for vice presidents for academic affairs, and faculty;
4. the Student Affairs track for vice presidents for student affairs, diversity, and inclusion specialists; and
5. the HBCU All-Stars track (by invitation only) for up to seventy-five HBCU all-stars and community organizers.

## ANNUAL REGIONAL HBCU SUMMIT ON RETENTION

The Annual Regional HBCU Summit on Retention (www.bowiestate.edu/hbcusummit) is a comprehensive conference that seeks the participation of students, faculty, staff, and administrators from colleges and universities across the region and nation. Each year, presenters share strategies and programs that can be adopted at institutions of higher education to improve student retention.

The summit aims to expand the collective knowledge of participants, share best practices, and strengthen efforts in recruitment, retention, and graduation. Collectively, attendees examine strategies, emerging technologies, and rapid changes on HBCU campuses to create ways to meaningfully engage students, providing uplifting paths to success as students are directed to take charge of their learning. The Annual Regional HBCU Summit on Retention is hosted in Ocean City, MD, in March of every year.

## NATIONAL ASSOCIATION OF STUDENT AFFAIRS ADMINISTRATORS IN HIGHER EDUCATION (NASPA)

The core of NASPA's (www.naspa.org) mission is to provide professional development for student affairs educators and administrators who share the responsibility for a campus-wide focus on the student experience. Professional-development programs at NASPA achieve this through a variety of conferences, workshops, and online learning opportunities, providing participants with access to the leading experts in higher education, student affairs, and other relevant fields.

The NASPA New Professionals and Mid-Level Administrators conferences are two national professional-development conferences hosted concurrently in June of each year designed to provide new and mid-level student affairs professionals with the opportunity to engage with colleagues and senior student affairs administrators and further develop their professional competencies.

The NASPA Annual Conference is held in March of every year. With more than eight thousand attendees, the 2015 NASPA Annual Conference hosted a record-breaking number of registrants, ranging from graduates to senior student affairs professionals. More than 1,750 institutions, from small to large campuses, four-year universities to community colleges, participated in the 2015 NASPA Annual Conference bringing together a diverse selection of higher education professionals from all fifty states and the District of Columbia, as well as twenty-nine countries.

## NATIONAL ORIENTATION, TRANSITION, AND RETENTION ASSOCIATION (NODA)

The mission of NODA (www.nodaweb.org) is to provide education, leadership, and professional development in the fields of college-student orientation, transition, and retention. NODA is an international association comprised of professional administrators, students, faculty, and related organizations that strives to attract pluralistic membership and leadership and endeavors to facilitate the professional development of its members.

The Annual NODA Conference focuses on how to elevate orientation, transition, and retention programs through innovation, while also rejuvenating a passion for serving new students and their families. In addition to regional conferences hosted throughout the year, the Annual NODA Conference is hosted at the end of October of each year.

## RUFFALO NOEL LEVITZ

Ruffalo Noel Levitz's (www.noellevitz.com) National Conference on Student Recruitment, Marketing, and Retention, hosted in July of every year, is the most comprehensive conference on enrollment management. Each year, presenters share successful strategies, new technologies, and campus programs that you can adapt to your own institution.

More than 120 sessions address topics such as: strategic enrollment planning, admissions, student success, student communications, campus marketing and positioning, financial aid, web and social media strategies, developing your staff, and technologies to improve enrollment efficiency.

Each year, thousands of college and university professionals participate in Ruffalo Noel Levitz conferences, workshops, teleconferences, and webinars including the Symposium on the Recruitment and Retention of Diverse Populations and the Strategic Enrollment Planning Executive Forum, both held concurrently in April.

## AMERICAN ASSOCIATION OF STATE COLLEGES AND UNIVERSITIES (AASCU)

AASCU (www.aascu.org) is a Washington-based higher education association of nearly 420 public colleges, universities, and systems whose members share a learning- and teaching-centered culture, a historic commitment to underserved student populations, and a dedication to research and creativity that advances their regions' economic progress and cultural development.

The AASCU supports institutional leaders by providing professional development that encourages exemplary practices and innovative management. The AASCU fosters innovation by promoting strategies that help members think deeply and creatively about the nature of their work and that encourage institutional achievement.

The AASCU creates professional development opportunities for its member presidents and chancellors, along with complementary programs and services for the presidential leadership team and for women and racial/ethnic minorities who aspire to leadership roles. The AASCU sponsors an annual Academic Affairs Winter Meeting each February, an annual Grants Resource Center Conference on Funding Competitiveness each February, an annual Communications Conference for Senior Professionals each March, the Millennium Leadership Institute each June, an annual Academic Affairs Summer Meeting each July, an annual Academic Affairs Summer Meeting, and the Annual Meeting of the AASCU each October.

## ASSOCIATION OF PUBLIC AND LAND-GRANT UNIVERSITIES (APLU)

Focused on increasing degree completion and academic success, advancing scientific research, and expanding engagement, the APLU (www.aplu.org) undertakes a wide array of projects and initiatives along with its members while providing a forum for public higher education leaders to work collaboratively to better meet the challenges and opportunities facing public universities.

The APLU Annual Meeting, hosted in November of each year, has become the premier event for public university leaders to meet and exchange ideas with colleagues from across the country and all of North America, learn about the latest challenges and opportunities facing public universities, and develop new ideas and initiatives to further strengthen their work.

The APLU Annual Meeting provides great opportunities to strengthen your institution along with ample networking opportunities—learn about best practices and share your institution's story.

As part of its ongoing effort to increase degree-completion rates, the APLU's Office for Access and Success and its Council of 1890 Universities host the HBCU Student Success Summit every June. This summit brings together HBCU presidents and chancellors, provosts, vice presidents for student affairs, enrollment managers, recruitment professionals, deans of students, advisement professionals, and student success professionals to learn about best practices and develop strategies to improve student success.

## THE COLLEGE BOARD

The College Board (www.collegeboard.org) is a mission-driven not-for-profit organization that aims to connect students to college success and opportunity. The College Board Forum is an annual gathering of K–12 and higher education professionals from all areas of expertise held in November every year.

The forum offers a wealth of sessions and workshops led by experienced colleagues that focus on finding solutions to today's most pressing education issues. The College Board's goals are to deliver opportunity to all students, to increase rigor, and to achieve equity and excellence in education.

The annual A Dream Deferred conference convenes in March of each year to discuss new solutions, share best practices, and collaborate with colleagues to make a difference for African-American students. College Board diversity conferences like A Dream Deferred are a key part of the College Board's mission to connect students to college success and opportunity.

A Dream Deferred is held in conjunction with the College Board's HBCU conference, a two-day professional-development event specifically designed for chief academic officers, deans or directors of admission, recruitment or enrollment management, and directors of financial aid at HBCUs.

## COMPLETE COLLEGE AMERICA

Established in 2009, Complete College America (CCA, http://complete college.org) is a national nonprofit with a single mission: to work with states to significantly increase the number of Americans with quality career certificates or college degrees and to close attainment gaps for traditionally underrepresented populations.

Through a mix of multistate reports, issue briefs, event presentations, and other resources, the goal of Complete College America is to help build widespread public understanding and support of the game-changers that will make it possible for all students to complete a credential or college degree. In October or December of each year, Complete College America sponsors an Annual Convening in conjunction with Complete College America Alliance of States.

## THE EDUCATION POLICY INSTITUTE (EPI)

The mission of the EPI (www.educationalpolicy.org) is to expand educational opportunity for low-income and other historically underrepresented students through high-level research and analysis. By providing educational leaders and policy makers with the information required to make prudent programmatic and policy decisions, EPI believes that the doors of opportunity can be further opened for all students, resulting in an increase in the number of students prepared for, enrolled in, and completing postsecondary education.

The Educational Policy Institute provides multiple levels of support for institutions of higher education to improve student success, including professional development, institutional consulting, research and policy analysis, specialized data tools for student success, and additional support through EPI's various free publications.

The Educational Policy Institute's Retention 101 Certification Workshop series offered throughout the year in different cities is designed for higher education leaders and practitioners interested in learning more about student retention and persistence issues, strategies, and solutions. The Annual EPI Forum on Education and the Economy is focused on the connections between the various levels of education and the workforce.

## NACADA: THE GLOBAL COMMUNITY FOR ACADEMIC ADVISING

Recognizing that effective academic advising is at the core of student success, NACADA (www.nacada.ksu.edu) aspires to be the premier global association for the development and dissemination of innovative theory, research, and practice of academic advising in higher education. NACADA promotes student success by advancing the field of academic advising globally through professional development, networking, and leadership for its diverse membership.

NACADA offers conferences, institutes, web events, and seminars throughout the year and in many locations, to provide quality professional-development opportunities for advisors, faculty advisors, administrators, and students who are invested in helping higher education students achieve academic success. In addition to the NACADA annual conference in October every year, NACADA offers annual summer institutes, administrators and assessment institutes, ten regional conferences, seminars, and symposia on current topics.

## CHAPTER 9: QUESTIONS AND NEXT STEPS

1. Identify one more national student success conferences for your participation.
2. Has internal or external funding been allocated to support the professional development of student success and retention administrators, faculty, and staff at the institution?
3. Submit a proposal for presentation at a global, national, or regional conference highlighting one of the successful programs or initiatives at the institution.

4. Register staff for webinars and local or regional workshops throughout the year, many of which are offered for free and eliminate the expense and inconvenience of travel.
5. Are new administrators, faculty, and staff afforded opportunities for professional development both on and off campus?
6. Network with colleagues at professional conferences by exchanging contact information and staying in touch throughout the year.
7. Collaborate with your peers at other institutions on future presentations, grant proposals and research, programs, and initiatives.

## REFERENCES

Hirt, J. B., Strayhorn, T. L., Amelink, C. T., & Bennett, B. R. (2006). The Nature of Student Affairs Work at Historically Black Colleges and Universities. *Journal of College Student Development, 47*(6), 661–76.

Jackson, J. F. (2001). *Retention of African American Administrators at Predominantly White Institutions: Using Professional Growth Factors to Inform the Discussion.* ERIC Database.

Nicholls, G. (2014). *Professional Development in Higher Education: New Dimensions and Directions.* London, UK: Kogan Page; Sterling, VA: Stylus.

Roe, E. (1986). Practical Reform and Utopian Vision—The Dialectic of Development. *J. Jones & M. Horsburgh. Research and Development in Higher Education, 8,* 18–28.

Zuber-Skerritt, O. (1992). *Professional Development in Higher Education: A Theoretical Framework for Action Research.* London, UK: Kogan Page.

*Chapter Ten*

# The HBCU Success Recipe

The Tinto model for student retention, first published in 1975, suggests that student attrition is the direct result of engagement between the institution and the student. The behavior of staying at college or leaving college from Vincent Tinto's model is the theoretical foundation of most student success and retention research and theory in higher education today.

The nine strategies discussed in this book—leadership, branding, data mining, frontloading, case management, strategic initiatives, leveraging external resources, technology, and networking—can increase retention and graduation rates by helping institutions to align programs and strategies for success with student-level variables such as student motivation, expectations, and goal attainment.

An author seeking to conduct a case study of student retention strategies at HBCUs found that there was not a lot of existing literature on the specific programmatic initiatives being implemented at HBCUs and that because institutional outcomes are not the result of any single attribute within an organization, examining factors that contribute to retention and graduation outcomes at HBCUs is worthy of critical analysis (Rahman, 2014). The success "recipe" for HBCUs is indeed a combination of programmatic initiatives, institutional factors, and student characteristics.

With a national six-year graduation rate of approximately 50 percent and an HBCU graduation rate of approximately 30 percent (NCES, 2011), institutions of higher education cannot afford to overlook or bypass the process of introspection that lends itself to the development of a comprehensive success model. Even as the nation rallies behind a college-completion agenda to promote postsecondary degree attainment, institutional level self-study should serve as the pith of any movement to promote student success.

## HBCUS AND THE COLLEGE COMPLETION AGENDA

In 2009, during his first address to the joint session of Congress, President Barack Obama stated that "by 2020, America will once again have the highest proportion of college graduates in the world. . . . So tonight I ask every American to commit to at least one year or more of higher education or career training. . . . Every American will need to get more than a high school diploma."

This speech resulted in the Obama administration's goal to have the United States lead the world in the proportion of twenty-five- to thirty-four-year-olds with two-year or four-year college degrees by the year 2020. Subsequently, the Obama administration established "state targets" for every governor outlining the total number of graduates that each state will produce by 2020 to help the nation meet this ambitious goal. These proposed state-by-state degree-production targets would yield a population of twenty-five- to thirty-four-year-olds with 60 percent degree attainment in the year 2020.

The Commission on Access, Admissions and Success in Higher Education, formed by the College Board, established the College Completion Agenda in 2009 with a goal to increase the number of twenty-five- to thirty-four-year-olds who hold an associate degree or higher to 55 percent by the year 2025 in order to make America the leader in educational attainment in the world.

According to the U.S. Census Bureau's 2010 Current Population Survey, as of 2008, 41.6 percent of twenty-five- to thirty-four-year-olds had attained an associate degree or higher in the United States. Currently, no state has a population of which 55 percent of its citizens have earned an associate degree or higher. And, as of 2008, only 30.3 percent of African-Americans age 25–34 had attained an associate degree or higher and only 19.8 percent of Hispanics age 25–34 had attained an associate degree or higher.

Harmon (2012) expounds that "Minority Serving Institutions (MSIs) including America's 105 HBCUs already are contributors to the national college completion goals and should be considered experts in the education of low-income, first generation, and under-represented students" (p. 8).

Morgan State University's twelfth president, Dr. David Wilson, has been very vocal about what he asserts is the critical importance of HBCUs and MSIs in helping the nation to achieve its higher education attainment goals. The data that forecast the characteristics of the college-going population in the years ahead project a more ethnically diverse, lower-income pool of students. President Wilson asserts this position in a recent editorial, *The Changing Face of Higher Education*:

> One of the advantages of the American system of higher education is that it has campuses with a diverse array of missions. The fact that many campuses have

liberal admissions standards makes it possible for flagship and other campuses to be highly selective while still allowing for society's broader needs for access to be met. The more selective institutions, however, typically are accorded the most prestige and the highest levels of public support because the perception is that selectivity is associated with quality. Based on past studies, it appears that only a small percentage of the emerging college-age population will have the credentials to be admitted to and succeed at these campuses. But what of all the other students?

## SHOULD HBCUS JUST ADMIT "BETTER" STUDENTS?

An Analysis of the Institutional Factors That Influence Retention and 6-Year Graduation Rates at Historically Black Colleges and Universities concludes that there is a relationship between institutional selectivity, faculty, and financial expenditures on graduation and retention rates (Lee, 2012). Marybeth Gasman reminds us that while HBCUs, on average, have a 30 percent graduation rate, it is important to keep in mind that most HBCU students are low-income, first-generation, and Pell grant–eligible students and are less likely to graduate no matter where they attend college (Mercer & Stedman, 2008).

It is accurate to state that the more selective HBCUs (i.e., Spelman College, Howard University, Hampton University, and Morehouse College) who enroll students with higher SAT scores have higher graduation rates than less selective HBCUs (Gasman, 2013). However, many public institutions such as Morgan State University officially have been designated by state legislatures as "access institutions" who are to offer access to a diverse population of citizens.

Unfortunately, while open enrollment and lack of selectivity at some HBCUs may support the access mission of the institution by affording opportunities to students who lack preparation or who have yet to demonstrate their potential, these relaxed admission standards also may undermine the institution in meeting strategic retention and graduation goals.

## BLAMING THE STUDENTS

Over the years, I have certainly attended my fair share of committee meetings. In fact, I have often jokingly referred to Morgan State University as "Meeting State University." The majority of these meetings have been highly productive; during many of these meetings I have observed a tendency for faculty, administrators, and staff often to blame only students for Morgan's retention and graduation challenges.

The default response to most discussions about student success, student learning outcomes, or student completion rates often has been: "We need to admit better students." Initially, I found that some administrators, faculty, and staff tend to focus on the shortcomings of students. Even the student members on many of our campus-wide committees participate in the "finger pointing" and the assignment of blame to student peers.

I do believe in personal responsibility and student preparation, but the answer to institutional challenges is not simply to admit students with higher SAT scores, higher GPAs, better precollege preparation, and/or higher household incomes. HBCUs historically have been mission-driven institutions, offering access to students who otherwise many have faced "closed doors." Therefore, increasing selectivity at HBCUs, especially public HBCUs, is a type of inherent contradiction.

At Morgan State University, I bring with me to every meeting data that demonstrates that whatever trend we may be observing in retention and graduation rates over the last twenty years is not the result of students "at the bottom" bringing the institution down, but rather our students with the highest SATs who were graduating at rates of 80+ percent presently are graduating at rates of 50+ percent, which has resulted in lower graduation rates for the entire undergraduate student population.

The students "at the bottom" of our student enrollment pool have had little to no fluctuation in their graduation rates over the past twenty-plus years, graduating at a rate above 30 percent, more than double the predicted rate for students with their academic and financial profiles.

These students "at the bottom" are the beneficiaries of our best student success interventions and strategies including a mandatory six-week summer bridge program, which has resulted in their consistent overperformance. It is imperative that we not slip into the trap of "blaming our students" for our institutional challenges, but instead recognize that Morgan State University has been successful in "doing more with less" and developing student potential at the top, as well as at the bottom, of the admissions pool.

## OVERCOMING THE IMPACT
## OF STUDENTS' FINANCIAL HARDSHIPS

It cannot be denied that students at HBCUs become acquainted with tremendous financial hardship(s) in their endeavor to complete a four-year degree in six years or less. This student quandary presents unique challenges for institutions. The lower household-income status of many African-Americans is highly correlated to their inability to pay for and to stay in college; it suggests the strong role that financial aid can play in recruiting, retaining, and graduating minority students (Seidman, 2005). Unfortunately, the financial circumstances of students at minority-serving institutions can be perceived as an "excuse" for institutional failures and low retention and graduation rates.

The Parent Plus loan serves as one distinct example of the negative impact of students' financial hardships on retention and graduation rates at HBCUs. The U.S. Department of Education has officially acknowledged the negative effect of the 2011 changes to Parent Plus loan-qualification standards on HBCUs. Specifically, at HBCUs the share of families with Parent Plus loans declined 46 percent, and the dollar amount of Parent Plus loans fell 36 percent, a decline more exaggerated than at other institutions (Arnett, 2015).

A report released by the U.S. Department of Education concludes that the adverse impact of changes to Parent Plus loan-qualification standards on HBCUs was significantly greater than the impact on other institutions, even when adjusting for income, and only one-tenth of the decline in Parent Plus loans at HBCUs was compensated with an increase in other types of federal loans.

The changes to Parent Plus loan-qualification standards resulted in an average of 3.4 percent decline in enrollment at HBCUs across the country, a larger decline than that experienced by other institutions in the same period (Arnett, 2015).

The Parent Plus loan changes provide one discrete example of the effect of students' finances on retention and graduation rates, but there are others. Chapters 5 and 6 of this book have detailed examples of financial barriers to degree completion for students at Morgan State University; the outcome at Morgan has been the development of strategic intervention strategies to mitigate the impact of these student financial challenges on the institution's student success model.

## GEORGIA STATE UNIVERSITY:
## THE "SUCCESS RECIPE" AT WORK

Georgia State University, a public, urban, minority-serving institution (MSI), has experienced the most dramatic increase in graduation rates in the United States, raising its graduation rate by twenty-two percentage points over the last ten years, from 32 percent to 53 percent. Georgia State University's more than twenty-four thousand undergraduate students receive federal Pell grants

(56 percent), are majority minority students (60 percent), and are 30 percent first-generation college students (Quinton, 2013). Georgia State was ranked tenth in the nation among institutions that surpass their predicted graduation rates based on student demographics on *Eduventures'* list of Top 25 Retention Performers.

Georgia State's university-wide commitment to student advising and attention to student progress to graduation have led to national recognition for creating innovative student retention approaches that foster the success of students from all academic, socioeconomic, racial, and ethnic backgrounds. Similar to Morgan's Starfish early alert and tracking system, Georgia State is one of a few large institutions nationwide that uses technology to track and monitor student progress from the moment that students arrive on campus until they graduate.

Another component of Georgia State's "recipe" for success is its program for first-year students that offers students (both those who live on campus and those who live off campus) the opportunity to participate in the university's Freshman Learning Communities to help ease the transition to college by clustering students who share common interests in the same class sections. "The university has found low-cost ways to give students more one-on-one attention, ranging from age-old peer tutoring programs to new data analysis" (Quinton, 2013).

In the same way as Morgan, once Georgia State University discovered that some students dropped out solely for financial reasons, running only a few hundred dollars short on tuition, "bridge grants" were offered to students to help them to stay at the institution (Burress, 2013).

*Learning from High-Performing and Fast-Gaining Institutions: Top 10 Analyses to Provoke Discussion and Action on College Completion* examines practices at Georgia State University and seven other fast-gaining institutions that have dramatically improved their graduation rates. When Georgia State initially tried to understand why the overall retention rates of 80–83 percent were not resulting in comparable graduation rates, they found that only 22 percent of freshmen were earning enough credits to foster sophomore status; instead they were earning an average of ten credits per semester instead of the fifteen credit hours per semester that research at other universities has suggested is a key milestone for college completion (Yeado, Haycock, Johnstone & Chaplot, 2014).

Listed in this comprehensive report were other components of the "success recipe" at Georgia State University, including:

• redesigning key courses and utilizing hybrid instructional models and supplemental instruction;

- establishing a post-freshman-year Summer Success Academy for the two hundred or so weakest first-year students, offering them an opportunity to earn another seven credits;
- bringing course redesign to their developmental math courses using 24/7 labs staffed by upper-level undergraduates;
- creating degree maps for more aggressive advising and early deadlines for students to declare a major so prerequisite and foundational coursework can be completed on time; and
- building very sophisticated data and tracking systems that continue to deepen understanding of what matters most and that automate many of the basic processes of monitoring student progress and triggering immediate human action when students go off track.

Georgia State University provides another case study where data mining, frontloading, case management, strategic initiatives, and technology serve as crucial approaches to increasing retention and graduation rates. As a public MSI, Georgia State has eliminated attainment gaps at the institution and has raised graduation rates of African-Americans at the same rate (or above) other racial and ethnic subpopulations.

The Georgia State University example is proof that the graduation rates of poor, first-generation students in need of remediation at public, urban universities can be improved significantly despite budget cuts and limited financial resources.

## WHAT WILL WORK: THE FUTURE OF RETENTION, PERSISTENCE, AND COMPLETION AT HBCUS

Chapters 1 through 9 of this book have outlined specific suggestions to promote student success and degree completion at HBCUs. Several comprehensive studies have been cited throughout this book that list recommendations for the future success of HBCUs. One such study is the 2012 UNCF study that used regression analysis to compare 85 HBCUs to 1,875 non-HBCUs; the authors recommended three specific strategies to improve retention and graduation rates at HBCUs: strengthening the K–16 alignment, expanding institutional student success measures, and enhancing college-access programs and student support services at HBCUs (Richards & Awokoya, 2012).

This particular study references a strategy not yet mentioned in this text, the alignment of the K–12 curriculum with postsecondary standards. This strategy should not go unrecognized; however, emphasis in this book has been placed on factors that are primarily internal to institutions.

The introduction of performance-based funding to the higher education landscape, and its pending adoption by many states, should not be interpreted as the "cure-all" or motivation for institutions to magically improve their completion rates. Instead, the preliminary results of states with performance-based funding can inform the decision-making process at institutions in terms of what will work at HBCUs in the future. For example, one study offers the following conclusions in reference to performance-based funding in the state of Tennessee:

> The introduction of retention and six-year graduation rates as a measure included in performance funding in 1997 did not result in a statistically significant difference in the mean retention or six-year graduation rates at Tennessee institutions compared to their peers. Additionally, the doubling of the monetary incentive associated with the retention and six-year graduation rate measures by the State in 2005 was not associated with increases in retention rates at Tennessee institutions compared to their peer institutions. These results suggest that States' adoption of performance-funding programs, such as the one in Tennessee, may not incentivize the change in institutional outcomes as desired by state leaders at their current funding levels. Based on the study's results, policy makers may want to: 1) consider increasing the financial incentives tied to these policies in order to elicit their desired change in institutional outcomes, or 2) consider other methods to improve institutional outcomes. (Sanford & Hunter, 2011, p. 20)

Ongoing changes in higher education most certainly will affect HBCUs. "The rapid pace of change in higher education affects every level of colleges and universities as performance measures move away from inputs such as the number of students, faculty, facilities, and programs toward outcome metrics that include retention and graduation, post-graduation outcomes (e.g., employment, graduate school, etc.), and the production of career-ready graduates" (Lee & Keys, 2013, p. 4).

In order for institutions to stay ahead of these anticipated changes, HBCUs must rise to the occasion by designing programs, implementing strategies, and creating innovative approaches to foster student success, increase retention and graduation rates, and duly promote degree completion.

## CHAPTER 10: QUESTIONS AND NEXT STEPS

1. Use this book and the nine recommended strategies to increase retention and graduation rates as a tool to foster student success and promote college completion.

2. Conduct a review of the literature and current research on student success strategies at institutions with similar characteristics to serve as a baseline for development of a student success model.
3. What data has been collected and evaluated at the institution to identify factors affecting retention and graduation rates?
4. Plan a meeting or retreat for campus partners and senior leaders to discuss the challenges facing the institution pertaining to retention, student success, and degree completion.
5. Who at the institution has the responsibility for oversight of strategies for student success and degree completion programs and initiatives?
6. Publish the results of your institution's retention and graduation programs and initiatives.
7. Share the vision for increasing retention and graduation rates with faculty, staff, and students, as well as with alumni, the community, and allies of the institution.

## REFERENCES

Arnett, A. (2015). ED Data Verify Damage Done to HBCUs. *Diverse: Issues In Higher Education*, April 23. Available at http://diverseeducation.com/article/71920.

Burress, J. (2013). Georgia State Univ. Improves Graduation Rates. *WABE, Atlanta's NPR Station*, May 2. Available at http://wabe.org/post/georgia-state-univ-improves-graduation-rates.

Gasman, M. (2013). *The Changing Face of Historically Black Colleges and Universities*. Philadelphia: Center for Minority Serving Institutions, University of Pennsylvania.

Harmon, N. (2012). *The Role of Minority-Serving Institutions in National College Completion Goals*. Washington, DC: Institute for Higher Education Policy.

Hughes, K. (2012). *The College Completion Agenda: 2012 Progress Report*. College Board: Advocacy and Policy Center. Available at http://media.collegeboard.com/digitalServices/pdf/advocacy/policycenter/college-completion-agenda-2012-progress-report.pdf.

Lee, J. M., & Keys, S. W. (2013). *Repositioning HBCUs for the Future: Access, Success, Research & Innovation*. APLU Office of Access and Success Discussion Paper 2013-01. Washington, DC: Association of Public and Land-Grant Universities.

Lee, K. (2012). An Analysis of the Institutional Factors That Influence Retention and 6-Year Graduation Rates at Historically Black Colleges and Universities. Available at http://hdl.handle.net/10161/5244.

Mercer, C. J., & Stedman, J. B. (2008). Minority-Serving Institutions: Selected Institutional and Student Characteristics. In M. Gasman, B. Baez, and C. S. V. Turner (Eds.), *Understanding Minority-Serving Institutions* (pp. 28–42). Albany: State University of New York Press.

National Center for Education Statistics (2011). Institute of Education Sciences, U.S. Department of Education, Integrated Postsecondary Education Data System (IPEDS).

Quinton, S. (2013). Georgia State Improved Its Graduation Rate by 22 Points in 10 Years. *The Atlantic*, September 23. Available at www.theatlantic.com/ education/archive/2013/09/georgia-state-improved-its-graduation-rate-by-22-points-in-10-years/279909.

Rahman, S. I. (2014). Spelman College: A Case Study of Student Retention Strategies. In F. Commodore (Ed.), *Opportunities and Challenges at Historically Black Colleges and Universities* (p. 27). New York: Palgrave Macmillan.

Richards, D. A. R., & Awokoya, J. T. (2012). Understanding HBCU Retention and Completion. Fairfax, VA: Frederick D. Patterson Research Institute, UNCF.

Russell, A. (2011). A Guide to Major US College Completion Initiatives. Available at www.aascu.org/policy/publications/policymatters/2011/collegecompletion.pdf.

Sanford, T., & Hunter, J. M. (2011). Impact of Performance Funding on Retention and Graduation Rates. *Education Policy Analysis Archives*, *19*, 33.

Seidman, A. (2005). Minority Student Retention: Resources for Practitioners. *New Directions for Institutional Research*, *2005*(125), 7–24.

Tinto, V. (1975). Dropout from Higher Education: A Theoretical Synthesis of Recent Research. *Review of Educational Research*, 89–125.

Wilson, D. (2015). The Changing Face of Higher Education. *The Baltimore Sun*, February 1, 2015.

Woolf, M. (2014). Who Leads the Rankings in College Football Retention Ratings? *Eduventures*, November 24. Available at www.eduventures.com/2014/11/leads-rankings-college-football-retention-ratings.

Yeado, J., Haycock, K., Johnstone, R., & Chaplot, P. (2014). *Learning from High-Performing and Fast-Gaining Institutions: Top 10 Analyses to Provoke Discussion and Action on College Completion*. Washington, DC: The Education Trust.

# Appendix A

## *List of Accredited HBCUs*

| INSTITUTION | WEBSITE | TYPE |
|---|---|---|
| Alabama A&M University | www.aamu.edu | four year, public |
| Alabama State University | www.alasu.edu | four year, public |
| Albany State University | www.asurams.edu | four year, public |
| Alcorn State University | www.alcorn.edu | four year, public |
| Allen University | www.allenuniversity.edu | four year, private |
| American Baptist College | www.abcnash.edu | four year, private |
| Arkansas Baptist College | www.arkansasbaptist.edu | four year, private |
| Benedict College | www.benedict.edu | four year, private |
| Bennett College for Women | www.bennett.edu | four year, private |
| Bethune-Cookman University | www.cookman.edu | four year, private |
| Bishop State Community College | www.bishop.edu | two year, public |
| Bluefield State College | www.bluefieldstate.edu | four year, public |
| Bowie State University | www.bowiestate.edu | four year, public |
| Central State University | www.centralstate.edu | four year, public |
| Cheyney University of Pennsylvania | www.cheyney.edu | four year, public |
| Claflin University | www.claflin.edu | four year, private |
| Clark Atlanta University | www.cau.edu | four year, private |
| Clinton Junior College | www.clintonjuniorcollege.edu | two year, private |
| Coahoma Community College | www.coahomacc.edu | two year, public |
| Concordia College–Selma | www.concordiaselma.edu | four year, private |
| Coppin State University | www.coppin.edu | four year, public |
| Delaware State University | www.desu.edu | four year, public |
| Denmark Technical College | www.denmarktech.edu | two year, public |
| Dillard University | www.dillard.edu | four year, private |
| Edward Waters College | www.ewc.edu | four year, private |
| Elizabeth City State University | www.ecsu.edu | four year, public |
| Fayetteville State University | www.uncfsu.edu | four year, public |

| INSTITUTION | WEBSITE | TYPE |
| --- | --- | --- |
| Fisk University | www.fisk.edu | four year, private |
| Florida Agricultural and Mechanical University | www.famu.edu | four year, public |
| Florida Memorial University | www.fmuniv.edu | four year, private |
| Fort Valley State University | www.fvsu.edu | four year, public |
| Gadsden State Community College | www.gadsdenstate.edu | two year, public |
| Grambling State University | www.gram.edu | four year, public |
| H Councill Trenholm State Technical College | www.trenholmstate.edu | two year, public |
| Hampton University | www.hamptonu.edu | four year, private |
| Harris-Stowe State University | www.hssu.edu | four year, public |
| Hinds Community College–Utica | www.hindscc.edu | two year, public |
| Howard University | www.howard.edu | four year, private |
| Huston-Tillotson University | www.htu.edu | four year, private |
| Interdenominational Theological Center | www.itc.edu | four year, private |
| J. F. Drake State Technical College | www.drakestate.edu | two year, public |
| Jackson State University | www.jsums.edu | four year, public |
| Jarvis Christian College | www.jarvis.edu | four year, private |
| Johnson C Smith University | www.jcsu.edu | four year, private |
| Kentucky State University | www.kysu.edu | four year, public |
| Lane College | www.lanecollege.edu | four year, private |
| Langston University | www.lunet.edu | four year, public |
| Lawson State Community College–Birmingham Campus | www.lawsonstate.edu | two year, public |
| Le Moyne-Owen College | www.loc.edu | four year, private |
| Lincoln University | www.lincolnu.edu/pages/1.asp | four year, public |
| Lincoln University of Pennsylvania | www.lincoln.edu | four year, public |
| Livingstone College | www.livingstone.edu | four year, private |
| Meharry Medical College | www.mmc.edu | four year, private |
| Miles College | www.miles.edu | four year, private |
| Mississippi Valley State University | www.mvsu.edu | four year, public |
| Morehouse College | www.morehouse.edu | four year, private |
| Morehouse School of Medicine | www.msm.edu | four year, private |
| Morgan State University | www.morgan.edu | four year, public |
| Morris College | www.morris.edu | four year, private |
| Norfolk State University | www.nsu.edu | four year, public |
| North Carolina A&T State University | www.ncat.edu | four year, public |
| North Carolina Central University | www.nccu.edu | four year, public |

| INSTITUTION | WEBSITE | TYPE |
|---|---|---|
| Oakwood University | www.oakwood.edu | four year, private |
| Paine College | www.paine.edu | four year, private |
| Paul Quinn College | www.pqc.edu | four year, private |
| Philander Smith College | www.philander.edu | four year, private |
| Prairie View A&M University | www.pvamu.edu | four year, public |
| Rust College | www.rustcollege.edu | four year, private |
| Saint Augustine's University | www.st-aug.edu | four year, private |
| Saint Paul's College | www.saintpauls.edu | four year, private |
| Savannah State University | www.savannahstate.edu | four year, public |
| Selma University | www.selmauniversity.org | four year, private |
| Shaw University | www.shawu.edu | four year, private |
| Shelton State Community College | www.sheltonstate.edu | two year, public |
| South Carolina State University | www.scsu.edu | four year, public |
| Southern University and A&M College | www.subr.edu | four year, public |
| Southern University at New Orleans | www.suno.edu | four year, public |
| Southern University at Shreveport | www.susla.edu | two year, public |
| Southwestern Christian College | www.swcc.edu | four year, private |
| Spelman College | www.spelman.edu | four year, private |
| St. Philip's College | www.alamo.edu/spc | two year, public |
| Stillman College | www.stillman.edu | four year, private |
| Talladega College | www.talladega.edu | four year, private |
| Tennessee State University | www.tnstate.edu | four year, public |
| Texas College | www.texascollege.edu | four year, private |
| Texas Southern University | www.tsu.edu | four year, public |
| Tougaloo College | www.tougaloo.edu | four year, private |
| Tuskegee University | www.tuskegee.edu | four year, private |
| University of Arkansas at Pine Bluff | www.uapb.edu | four year, public |
| University of Maryland Eastern Shore | www.umes.edu | four year, public |
| University of the District of Columbia | www.udc.edu | four year, public |
| University of the Virgin Islands | www.uvi.edu | four year, public |
| University of the Virgin Islands–Kingshill | www.uvi.edu | four year, public |
| Virginia State University | www.vsu.edu | four year, public |
| Virginia Union University | www.vuu.edu | four year, private |
| Virginia University of Lynchburg | www.vul.edu | four year, private |
| Voorhees College | www.voorhees.edu | four year, private |
| West Virginia State University | www.wvstateu.edu | four year, public |
| Wilberforce University | www.wilberforce.edu | four year, private |

| INSTITUTION | WEBSITE | TYPE |
|---|---|---|
| Wiley College | www.wileyc.edu | four year, private |
| Winston-Salem State University | www.wssu.edu | four year, public |
| Xavier University of Louisiana | www.xula.edu | four year, private |

**Taken from the White House Initiative on Historically Black Colleges and Universities list of accredited HBCUs: www.ed.gov/edblogs/whhbcu/one-hundred-and-five-historically-black-colleges-and-universities.

# Appendix B
## *Notable Morgan State University Alumni*

| Name | Class Year | Accomplishments |
|---|---|---|
| Kenneth Alston | 2006 | Counter-tenor and accomplished singer; star of Broadway musical *Three Mo Tenors* |
| Robert M. Bell | 1966 | First African-American chief justice of the Maryland Court of Appeals |
| Joe Black | 1950 | Negro League and Major League baseball pitcher; first African-American pitcher to win a World Series (1952) |
| Clarence Blount | 1950 | Buffalo soldier in WWII in the 92nd infantry; the first African-American to serve as Senate majority leader in Maryland; educator and civic activist |
| Roosevelt Brown | 1953 | NFL player and member of the Professional Football Hall of Fame |
| Joe Clair | 1992 | Comedian and radio and TV show host; five years as host of BET's *Rap City* |
| Harry Cole | 1943 | First African-American member of the Maryland State Senate |
| Josh Culbreath | 1955 | 1956 summer Olympic bronze medalist in the 400 meter hurdles |
| Jae Deal | 2002 | Composer and music producer |
| Richard Dixon | 1960 | Maryland state treasurer; first African-American treasurer; member of the Maryland General Assembly |
| Terry Edmonds | 1973 | First African-American speechwriter in the White House; chief speechwriter for President William Jefferson Clinton |
| Larry Ellis | 1969 | Four-star general and former Commander of the U.S. Army Forces Command; recipient of medals of honor |

| Name | Class Year | Accomplishments |
| --- | --- | --- |
| Len Ford | 1949 | NFL player and member of the Professional Football Hall of Fame |
| Wilson Goode | 1961 | First African-American mayor of the city of Philadelphia |
| Earl G. Graves | 1957 | Entrepreneur; founder of *Black Enterprise Magazine*; former chairman and CEO of Pepsi Cola of Washington, DC, LP |
| Peter Harvey | 1979 | First African-American to serve as attorney general for the state of New Jersey |
| Solomon Howard | 2009 | Opera singer; performed with the Metropolitan Opera, the Washington National Opera, and the L.A. Opera |
| Zora Neale Hurston | 1918 | Harlem Renaissance writer known for *Their Eyes Were Watching God* |
| Mo'Nique Imes | 1987 | Academy Award–winning actress and comedian; star of the movie *Precious* |
| Leroy Kelly | 1963 | NFL player and member of the Professional Football Hall of Fame |
| Willie Lanier | 1966 | NFL player and member of the Professional Football Hall of Fame |
| Maysa Leak | 1991 | Grammy Award–nominated smooth jazz singer |
| Kevin Liles | Attended 1986–1989 | Former president of Def Jam Entertainment and executive vice president of Warner Music Group; founder of KWL Enterprises, an artist management company; author of *Make It Happen: Hip Hop Guide to Success* |
| Nathaniel McFadden | 1968 | State senator and former Senate majority leader in Maryland |
| Kweisi Mfume | 1976 | Former five-term Maryland congressman and chair of the Congressional Black Caucus; former president and CEO of the NAACP |
| Parren J. Mitchell | 1950 | WWII Purple Heart medalist; first African-American member of the U.S. Congress in Maryland |
| Margaret Murphy | 1977 | Maryland House of Delegates member; first African-American female chairman of the Baltimore City Delegation |
| Catherine Pugh | 1973 | State senator in Maryland |
| Howard "Pete" Rawlings | 1969 | First African-American to become chair of the Appropriations Committee in the Maryland House of Delegates |
| William C. Rhoden | 1972 | *New York Times* columnist |
| Keith L. Russell | 1995 | *Action News* weekend sport anchor |

| Name | Class Year | Accomplishments |
| --- | --- | --- |
| April Ryan | 1989 | Journalist serving as White House correspondent for American Urban Radio Networks through multiple presidential administrations; author of *The Presidency in Black and White: My Up-Close View of Three Presidents and Race in America* |
| Elijah Saunders | 1956 | Founding member of the Association of Black Cardiologists; awarded the American Heart Association Award of Merit, the highest honor in the field |
| Lonnie Liston Smith | 1961 | American jazz artist |
| Rochelle Stevens | 1988 | Olympic gold and silver medalist in track and field |
| David E. Talbert | 1989 | NAACP Award–winning playwright and author; writer of "black plays"; producer and director of movies such as *First Sunday* and *Baggage Claim* |
| William "Kip" Ward | 1971 | Four-star general in the U.S. Army; former commander of the U.S. Africa Command |
| Marvin Webster | 1974 | NBA player known as the "Human Eraser" |
| Verda Welcome | 1939 | First African-American woman elected to the Maryland State Senate |
| Deniece Williams | Attended 1968–1970 | Grammy Award–winning artist and writer of hit song "Let's Hear it for the Boy" |
| Sam Art Williams | 1968 | Writer and producer of famous television shows such as *Martin* and *The Fresh Prince of Bel-Air* |